"Our bodies were
printed as blank pages
to be filled with the
ink of our hearts."

Michael Biondi

INKED

LOLA MARS

INKED

Summersdale Publishers Ltd
46 West Street
Chichester
West Sussex
PO19 1RP
UK

www.summersdale.com

Printed and bound in China

ISBN: 978-1-84953-725-4

Substantial discounts on bulk quantities of Summersdale books are available to corporations, professional associations and other organisations. For details contact Nicky Douglas by telephone: +44 (0) 1243 756902, fax: +44 (0) 1243 786300 or email: nicky@summersdale.com.

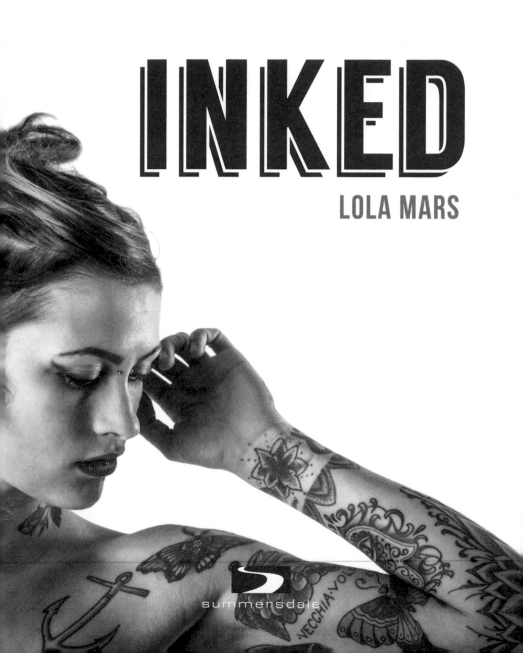

INKED

LOLA MARS

summersdale

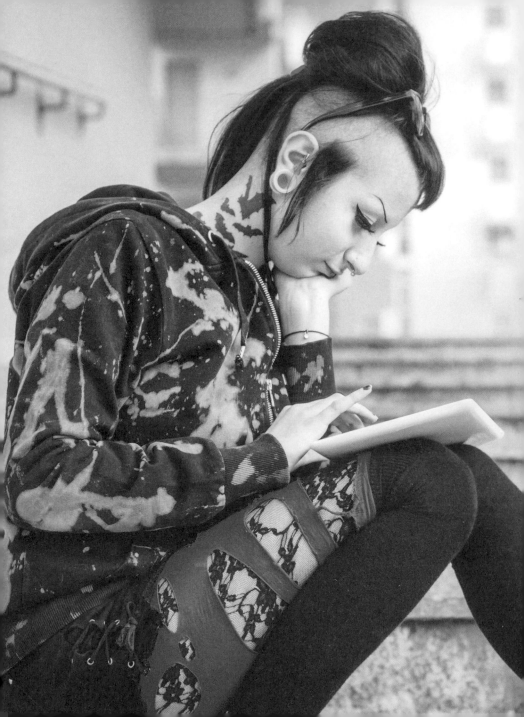

Introduction

Tattoos are art; and an art form at the peak of groundbreaking innovation at that. *Inked* celebrates the new-wave tattooists and body artists, while doffing our caps to the classic styles that paved the way to the surge of creativity and invention found in contemporary tattoo art. Simple outlines and a limited palette have exploded into watercolours, photorealism and pen-and-ink works of art. With new technology and cutting-edge techniques, a tattoo artist can create unique and exquisite pieces with as much freedom as an expressionist painter. Now body art can be gorgeously vibrant or meticulously detailed; shaded with jumping-off-the-skin 3D tangibility or stunning in its black-and-white simplicity. I hope you enjoy flicking through these pages and finding inspiration for your next tattoo, or simply looking in awe at these incredible examples of today's best body artists at work.

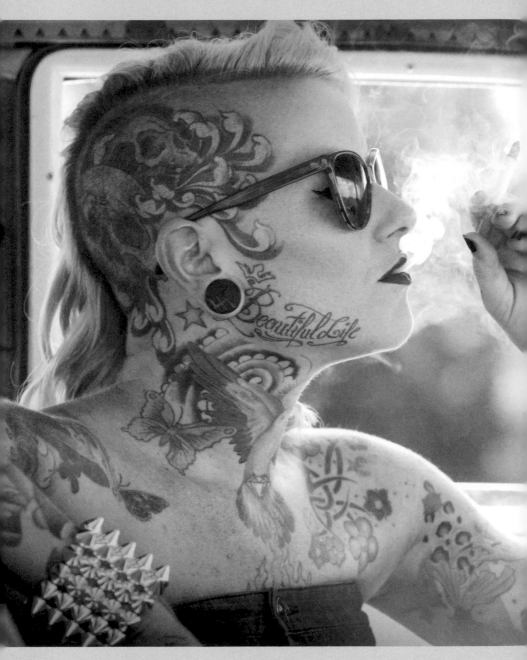

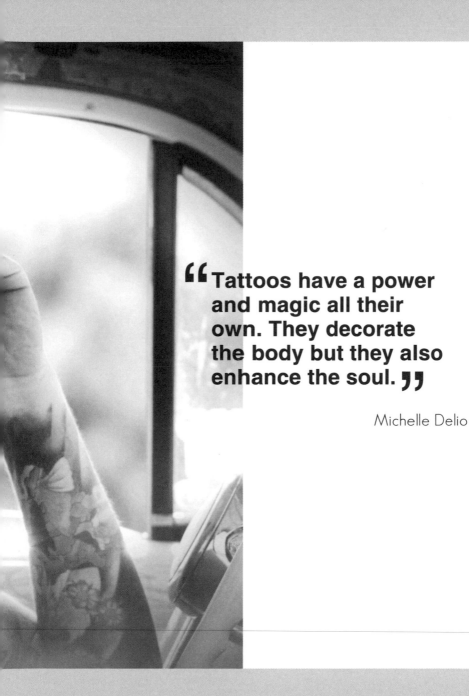

"Tattoos have a power and magic all their own. They decorate the body but they also enhance the soul. "

Michelle Delio

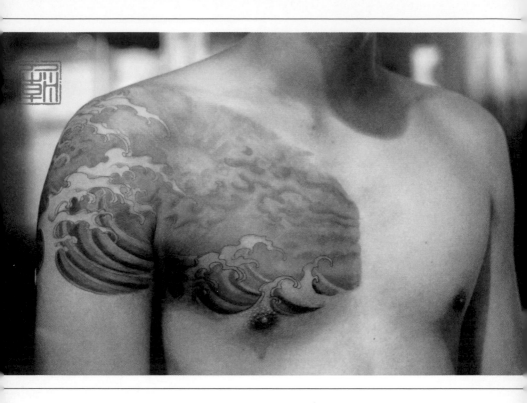

On life's vast ocean diversely
we sail. Reasons the card, but
passion the gale.

Alexander Pope

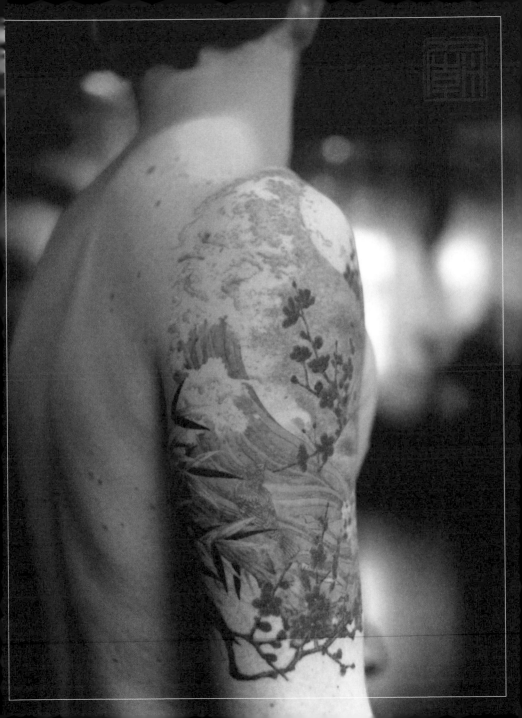

"If the body is a temple,
then tattoos are its
stained-glass windows."

Vince Hemingson

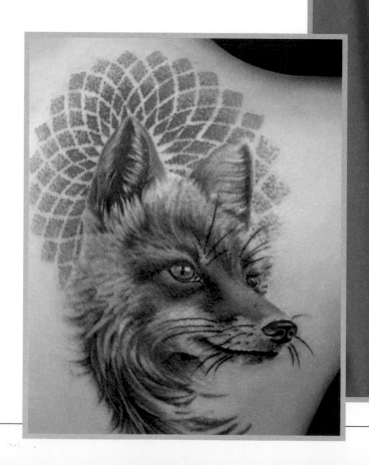

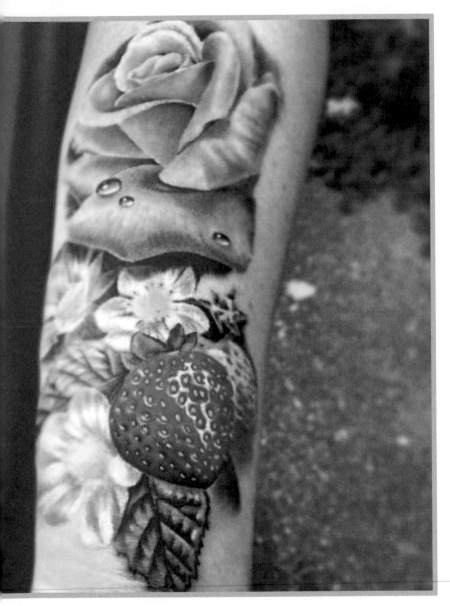

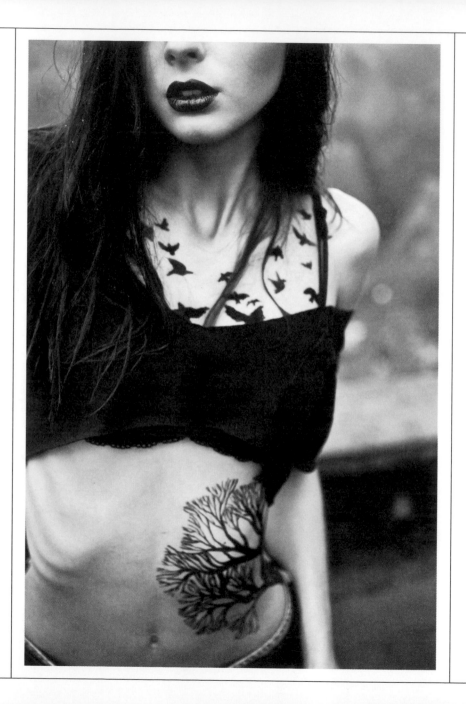

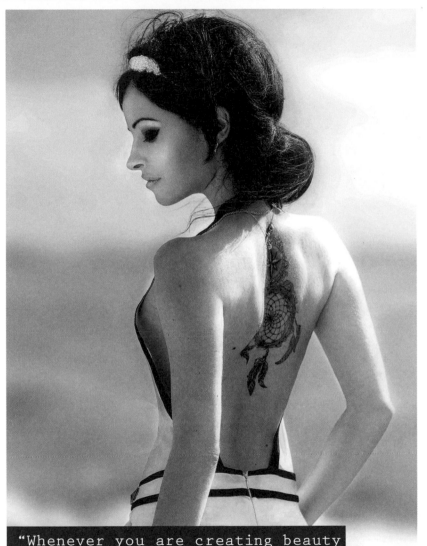

"Whenever you are creating beauty around you, you are restoring your own soul."

Alice Walker

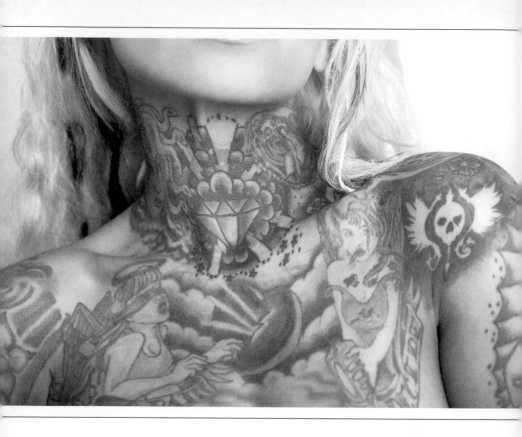

To change one's life:
Start immediately.
Do it flamboyantly.
No exceptions.

William James

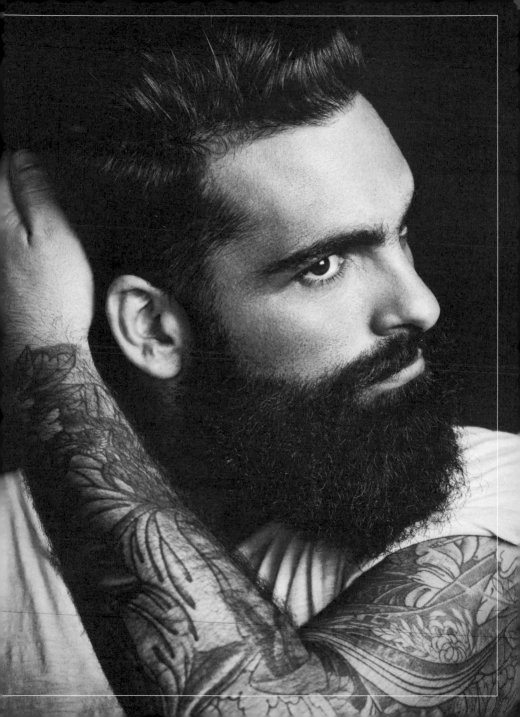

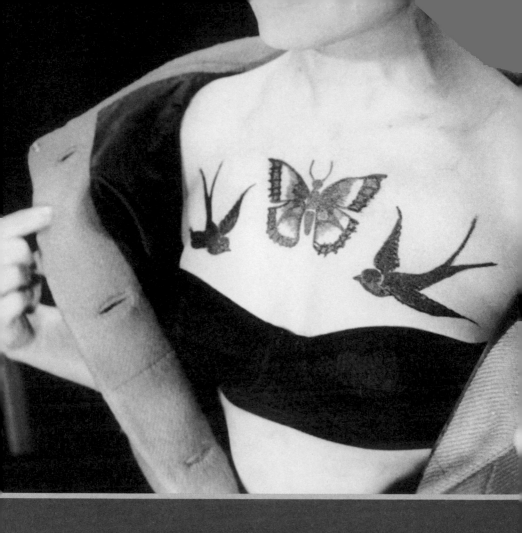

"Freedom is the
oxygen of the soul."

Moshe Dayan

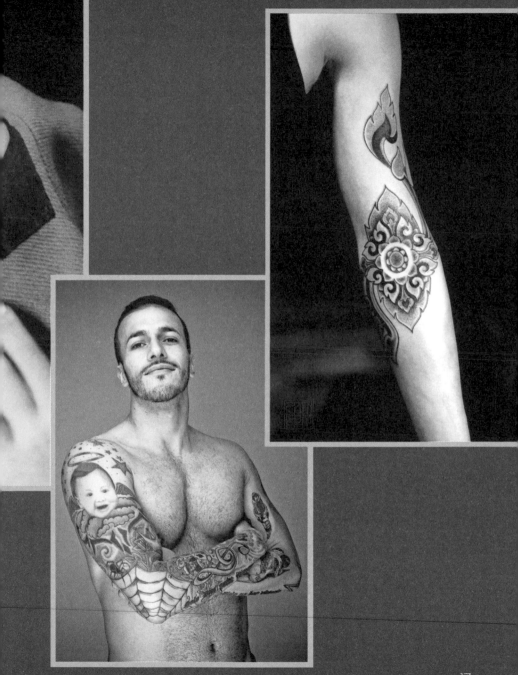

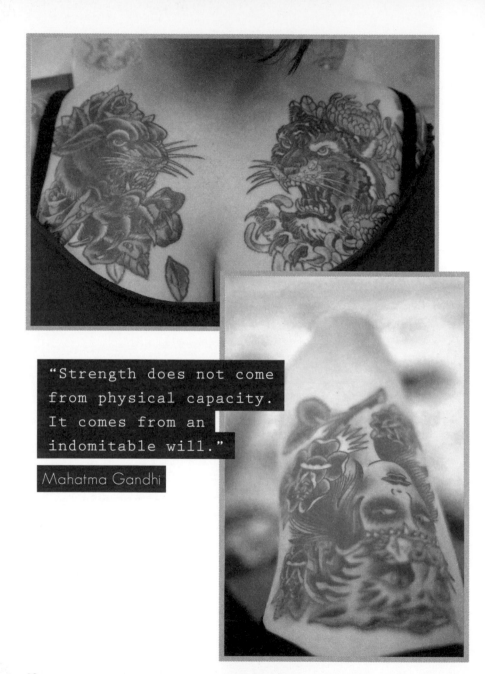

"Strength does not come from physical capacity. It comes from an indomitable will."

Mahatma Gandhi

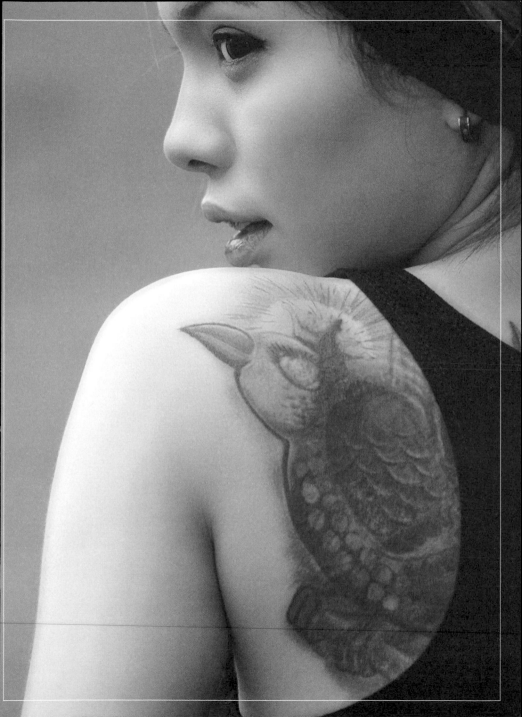

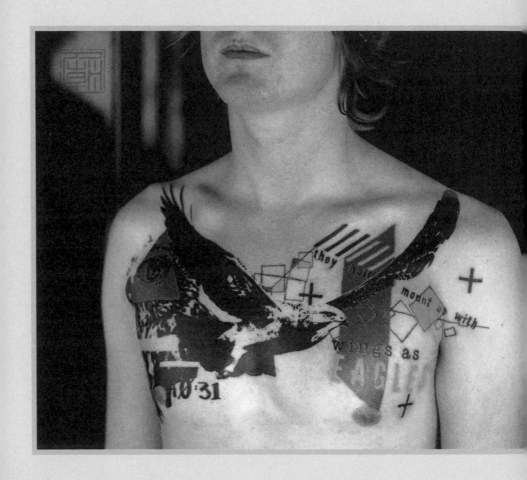

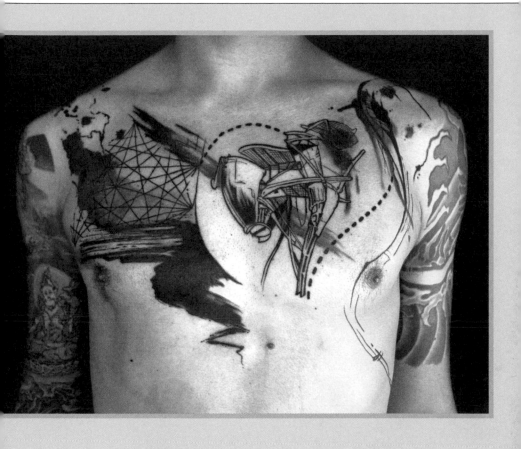

"Freedom lies in being bold."

Robert Frost

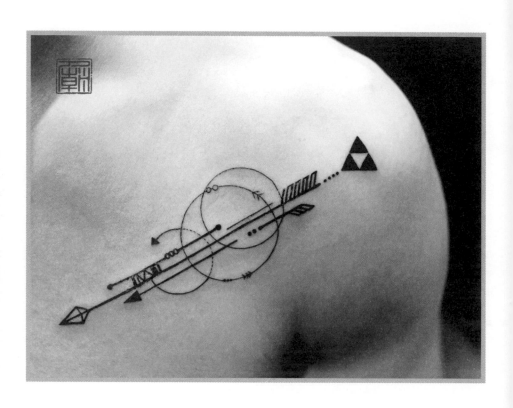

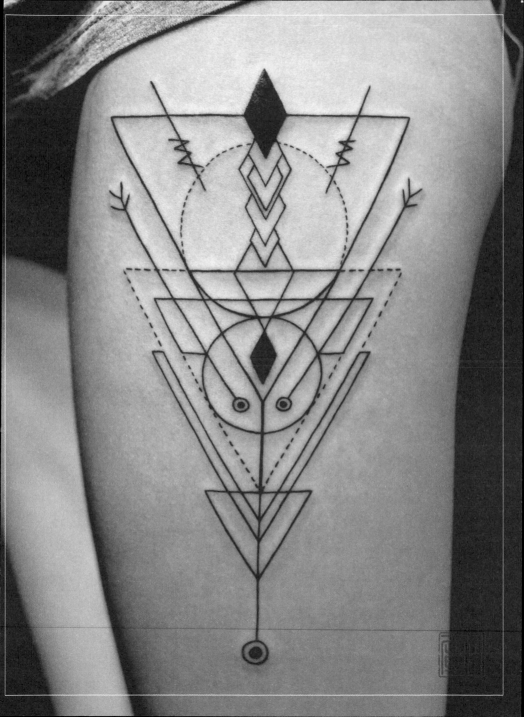

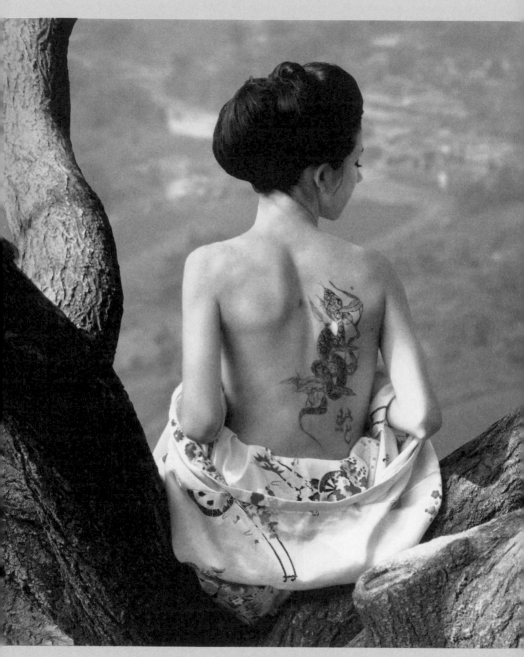

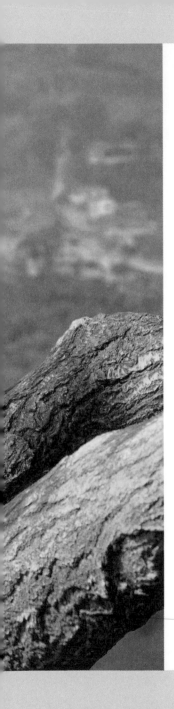

❝To blossom forth, a work of art must ignore or rather forget all the rules.❞

Pablo Picasso

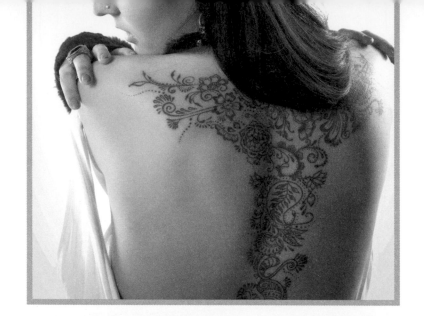

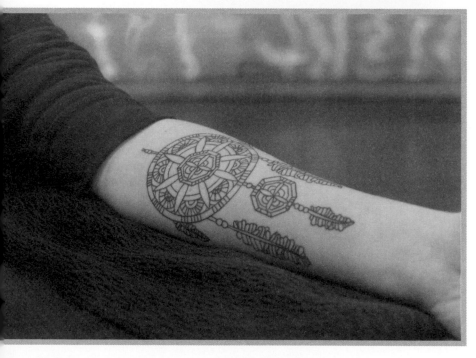

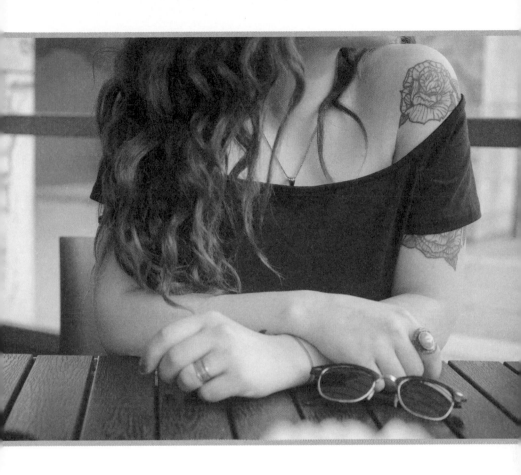

"There is only one way to avoid criticism:
do nothing, say nothing, and be nothing."

Aristotle

66

Be yourself; everyone else is already taken.

Oscar Wilde

99

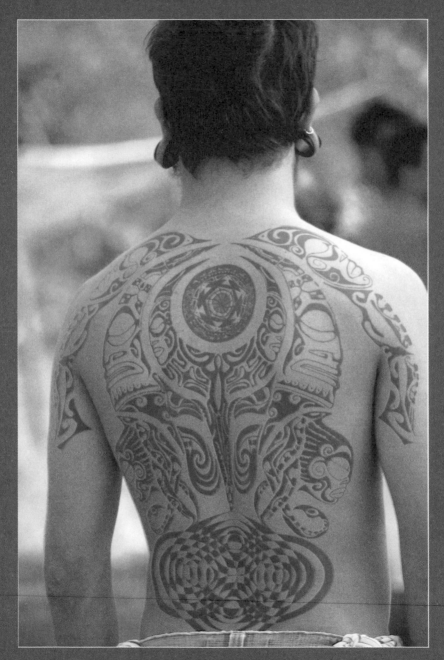

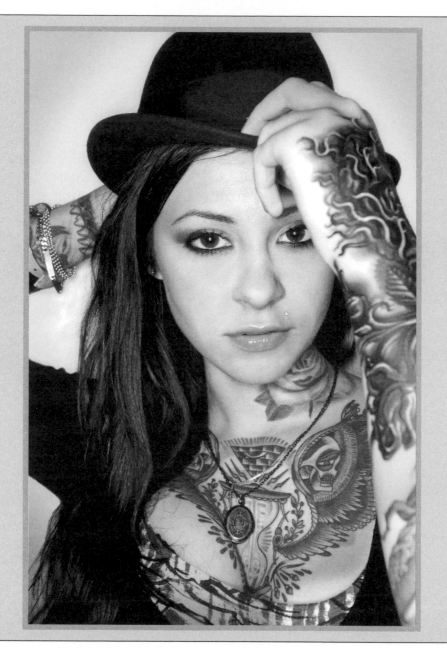

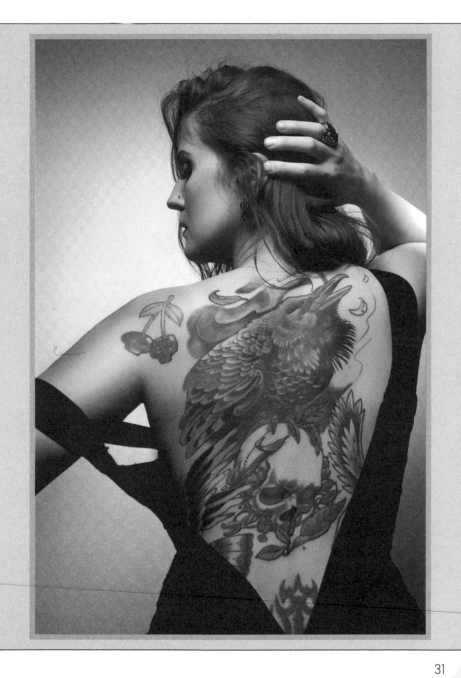

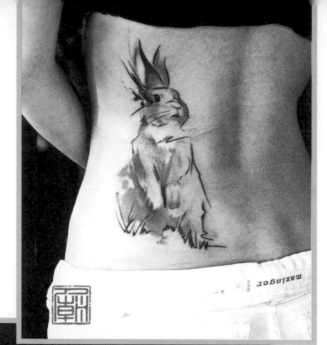

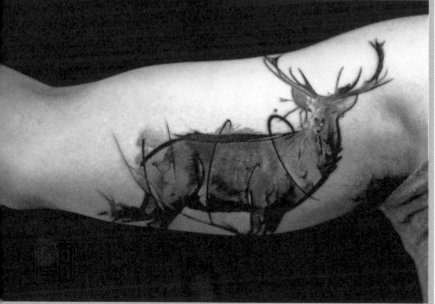

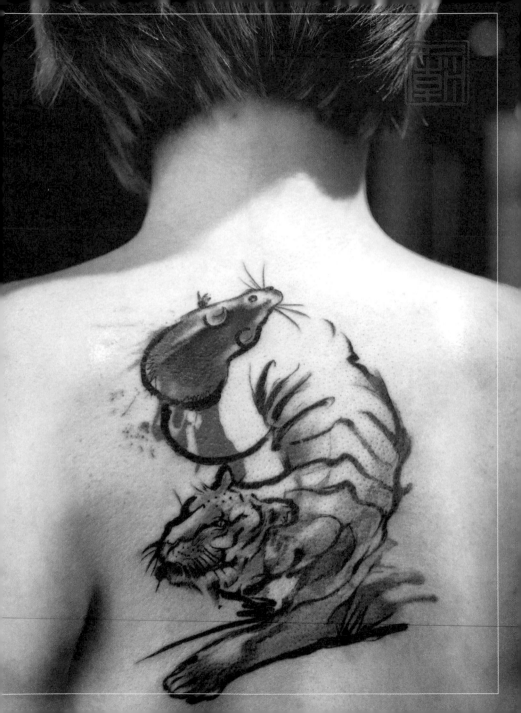

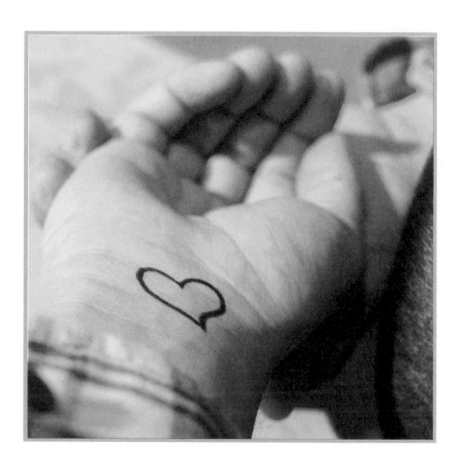

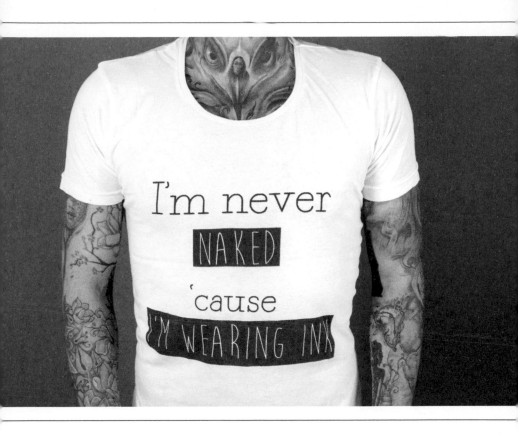

> Wear your heart on your skin in this life.

Sylvia Plath

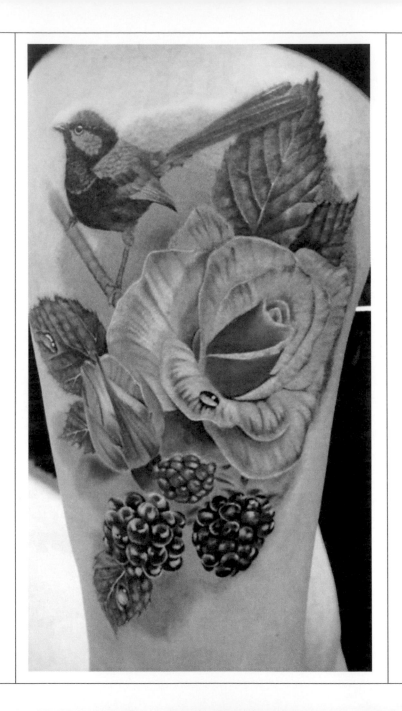

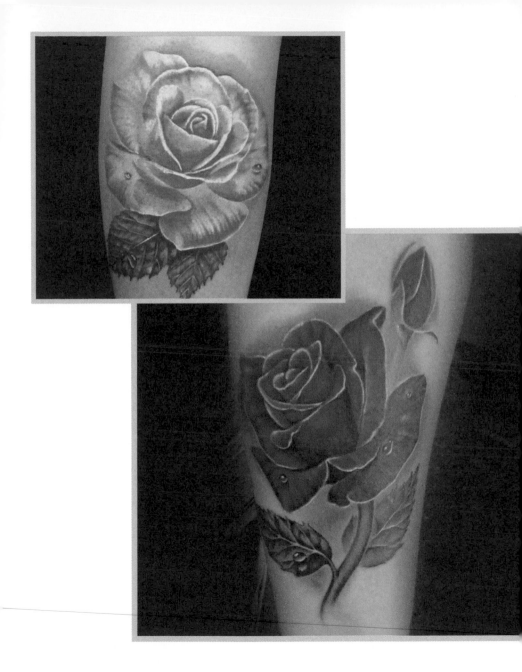

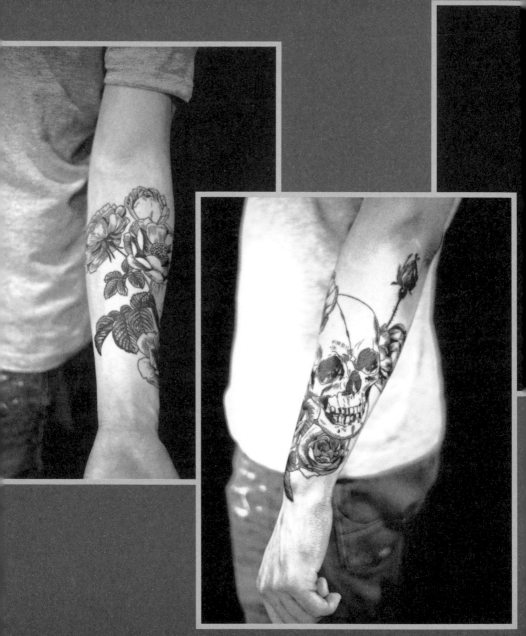

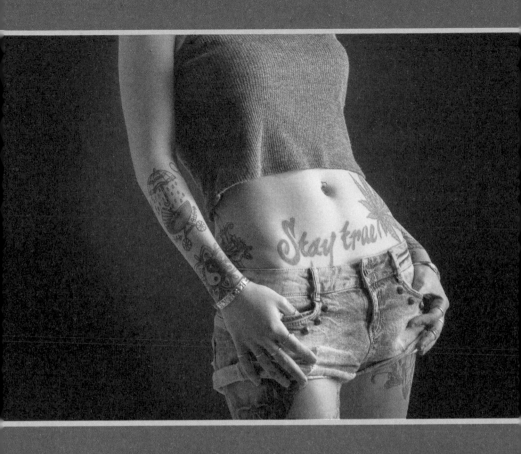

"Be yourself. The world
worships the original."

Ingrid Bergman

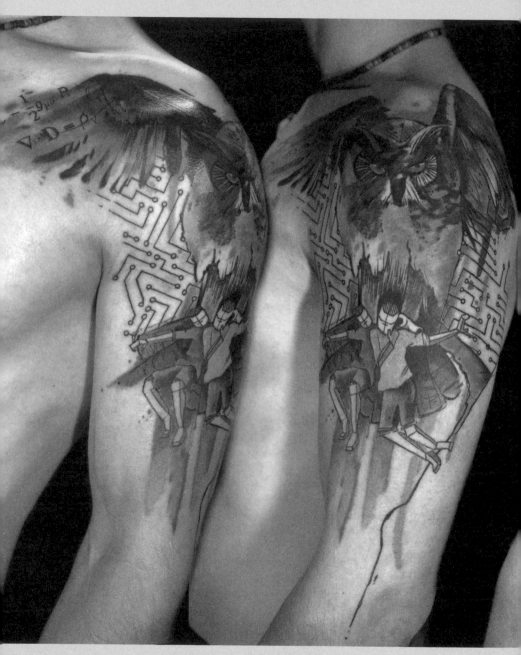

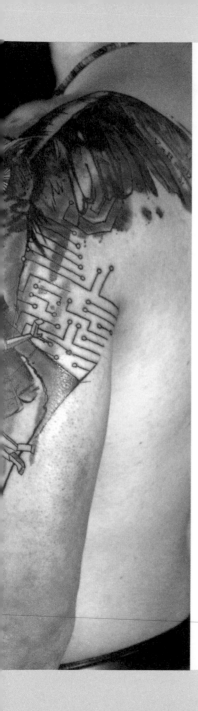

"Tattoos exude pain and pleasure all at the same time."

Chester Bennington

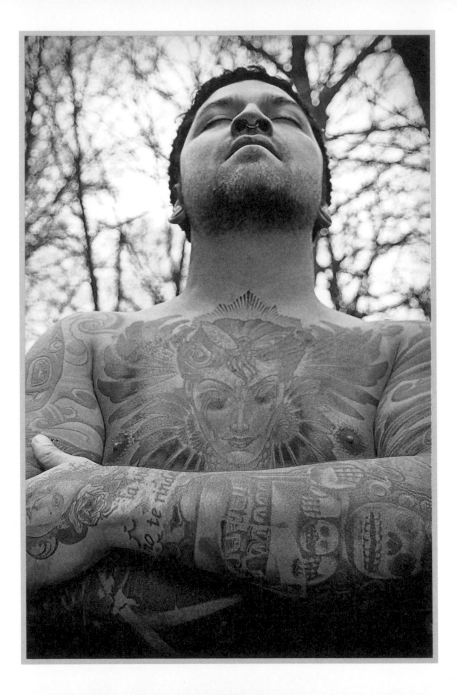

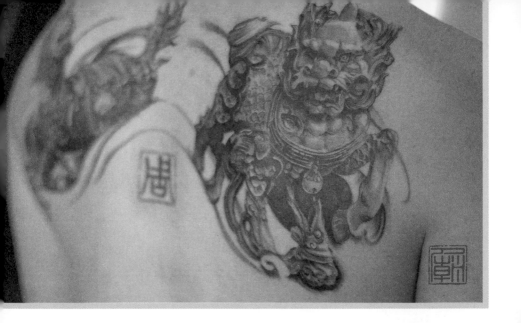

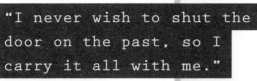

"I never wish to shut the door on the past, so I carry it all with me."

Dave Navarro

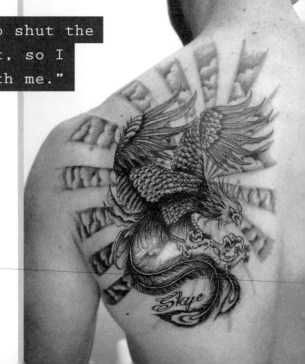

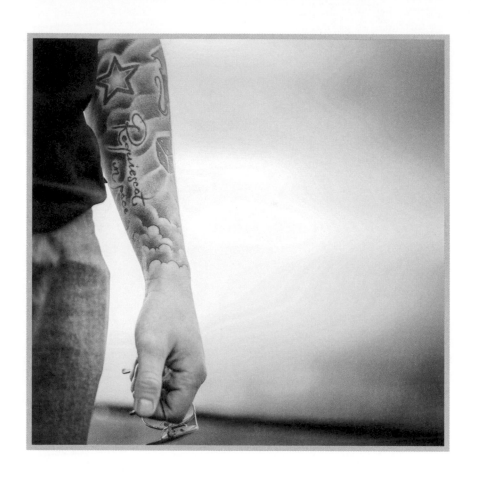

"There is no way to happiness -
happiness is the way."

Thích Nhất Hạnh

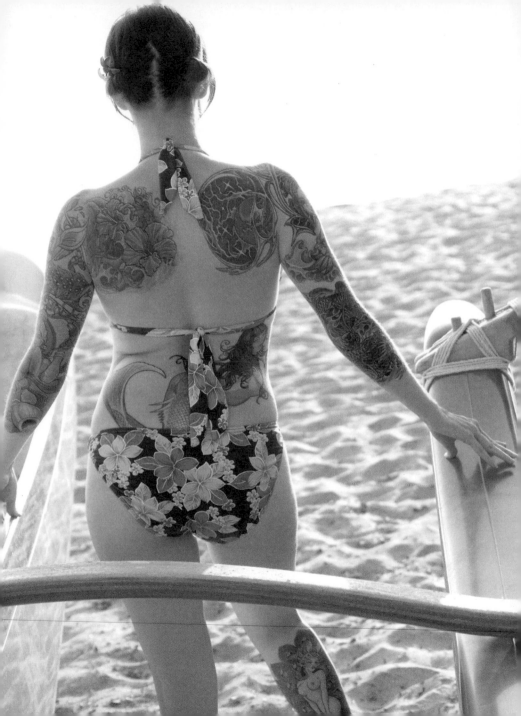

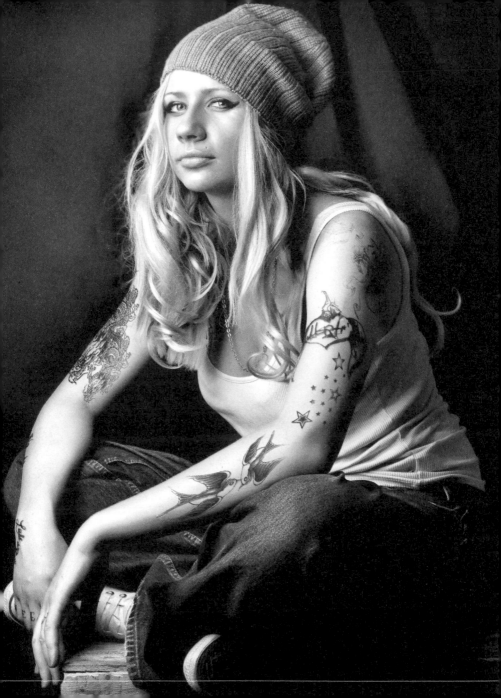

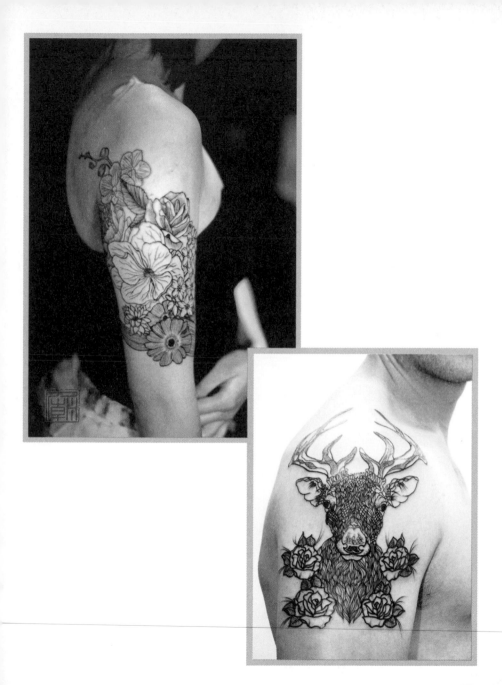

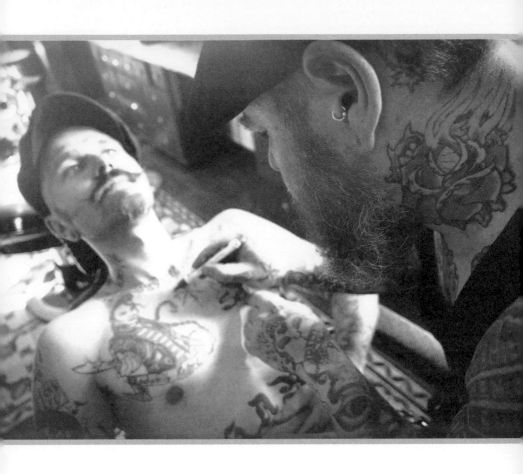

"My story is etched in lines and shading,
and you can read it on my arms, my
legs, my shoulders and my stomach."

Kat Von D

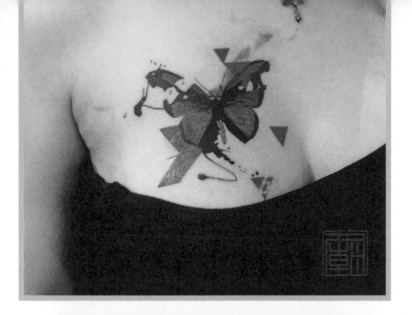

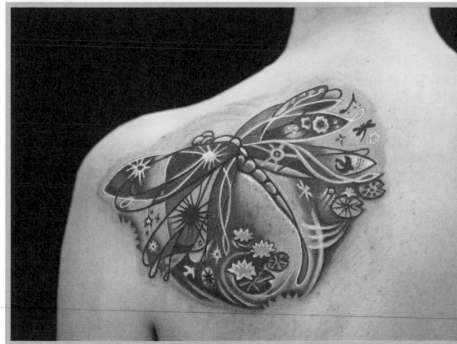

49

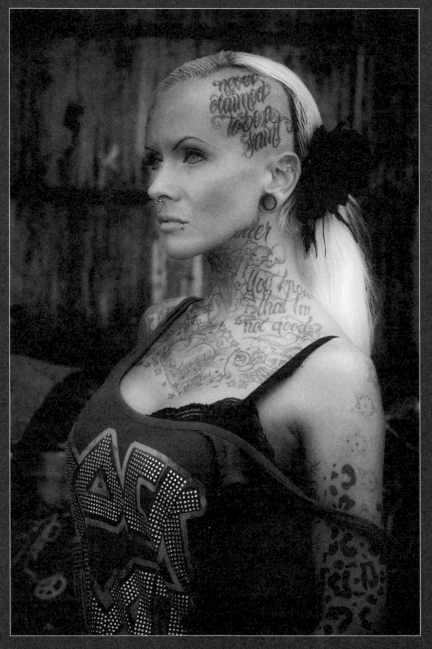

***The universe has
no restrictions.***

Deepak Chopra

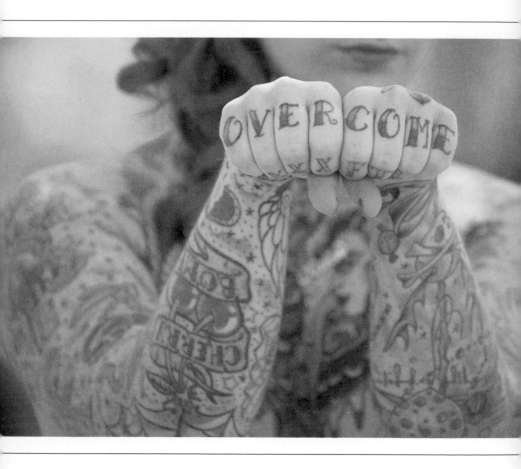

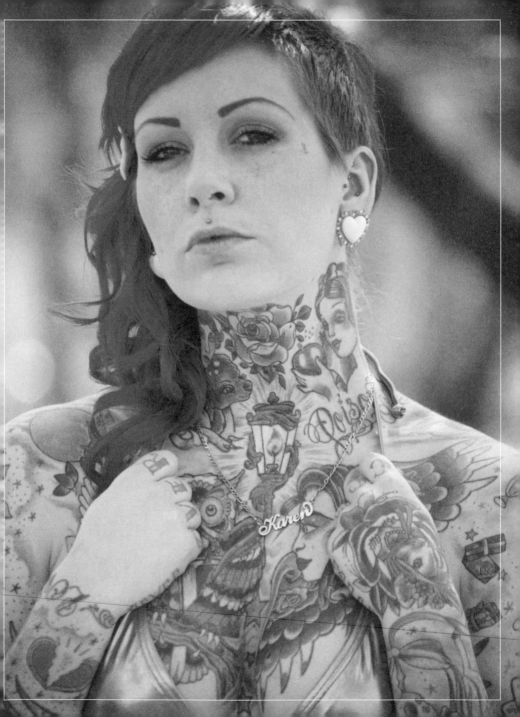

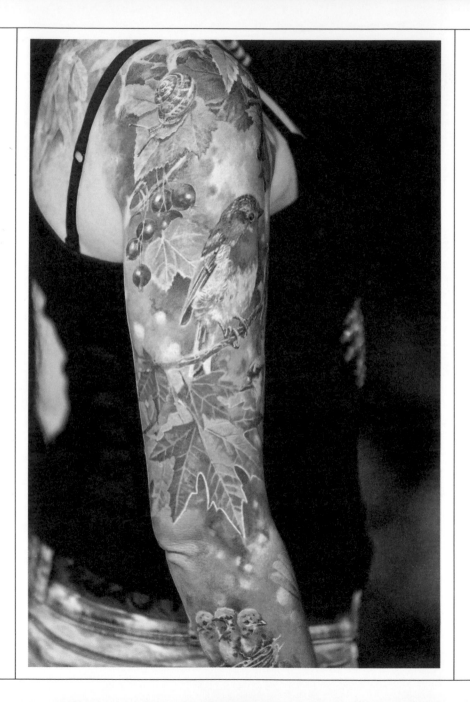

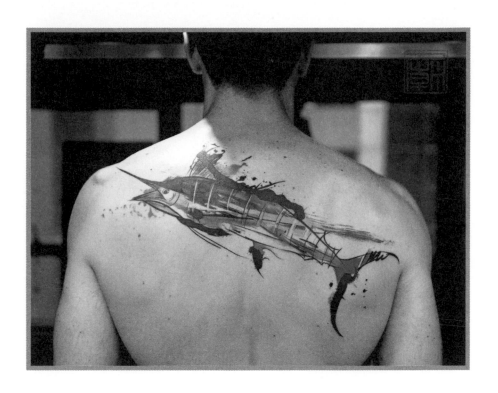

Live in the sunshine, swim the sea,
drink the wild air's salubrity.

Ralph Waldo Emerson

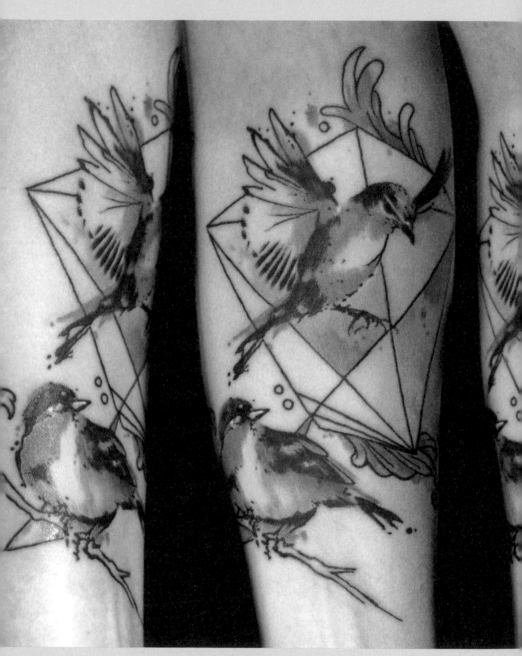

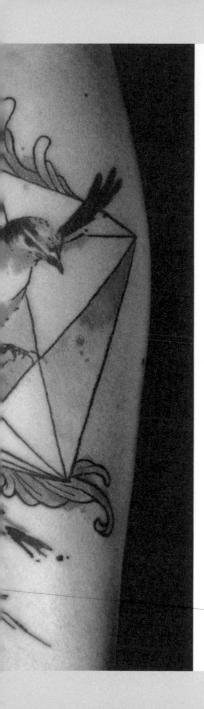

" Character may be manifested in the great moments, but it is made in the small ones. ""

Phillips Brooks

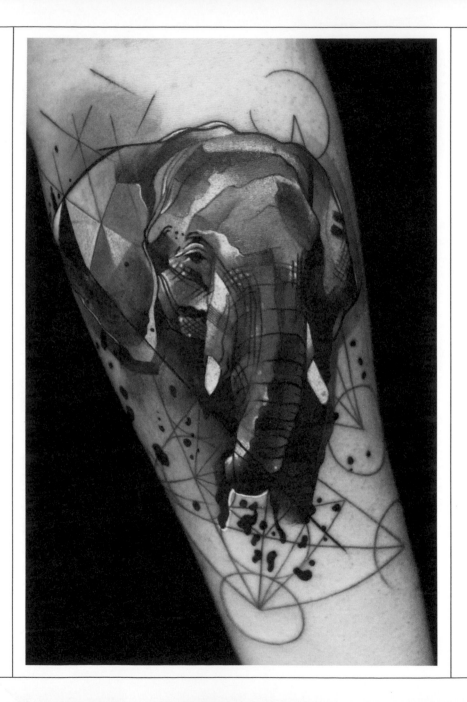

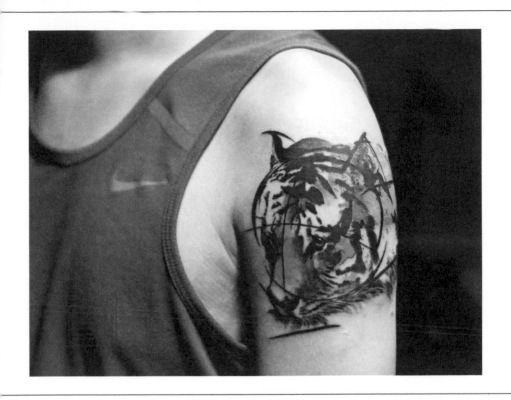

"
He who loves, flies, runs
and rejoices; he is free and
nothing holds him back.

Henri Matisse
"

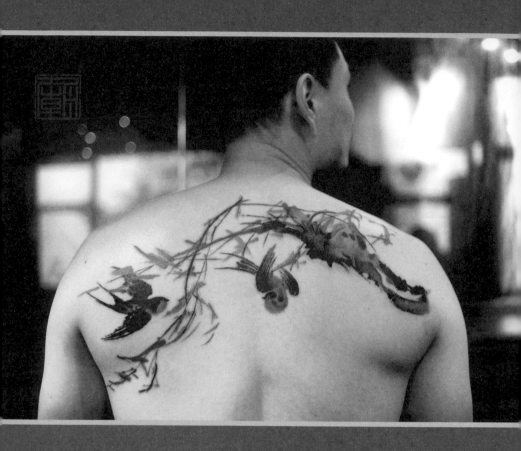

"Show me a man with a tattoo
and I'll show you a man with an
interesting past."

Jack London

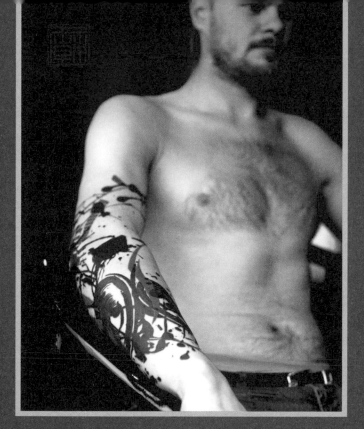

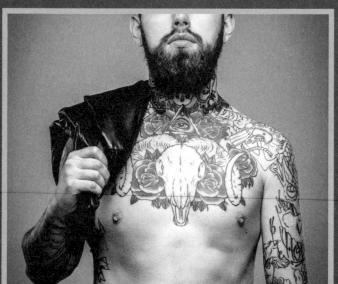

61

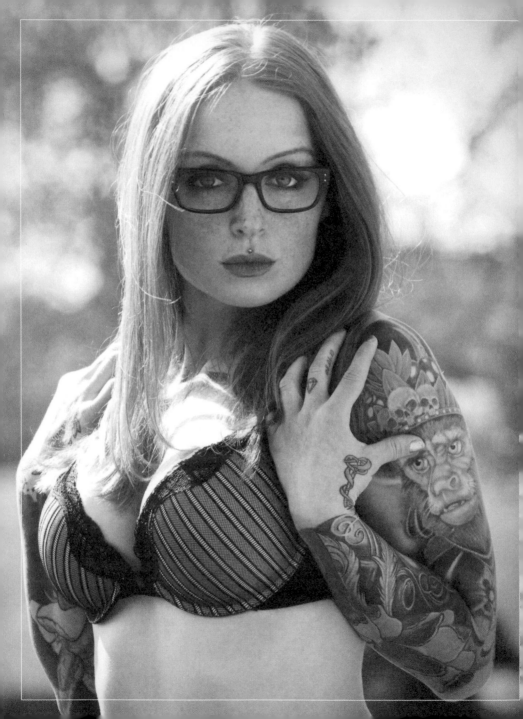

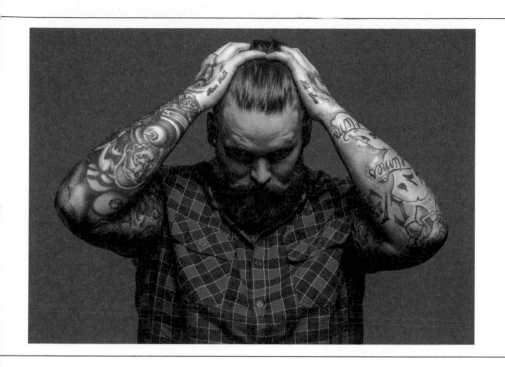

There are dark shadows on
the earth, but its lights are
stronger in the contrast.

Charles Dickens

"Imagination is the
eye of the soul."

Joseph Joubert

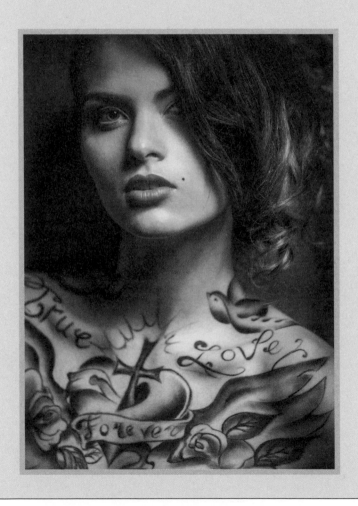

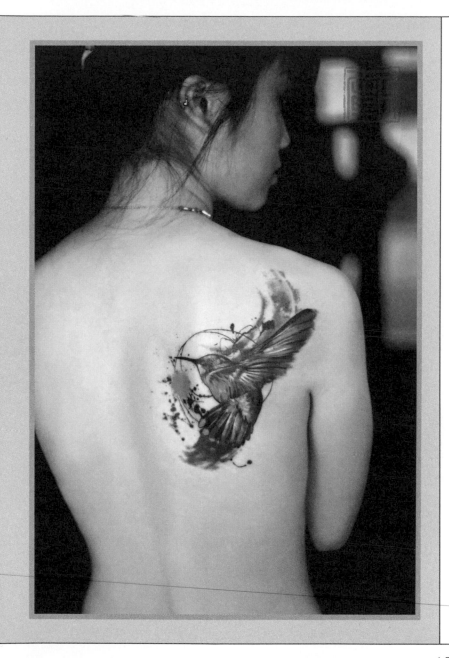

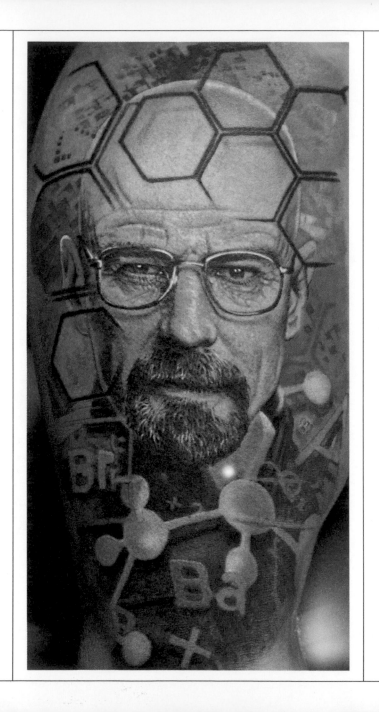

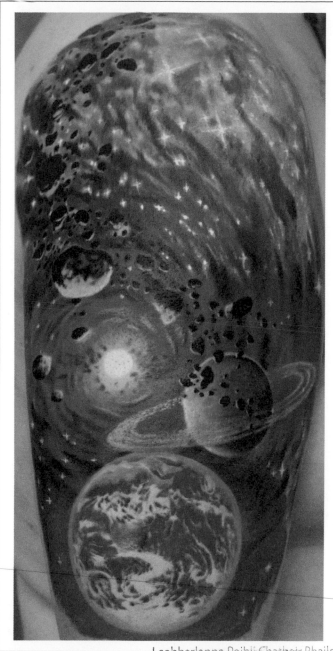

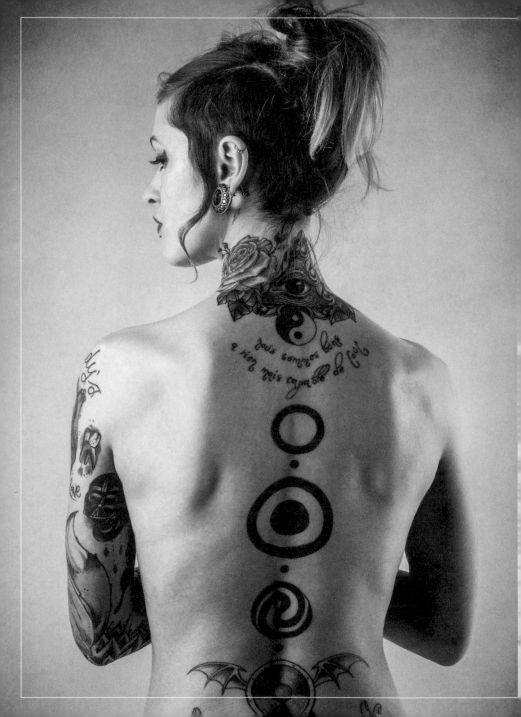

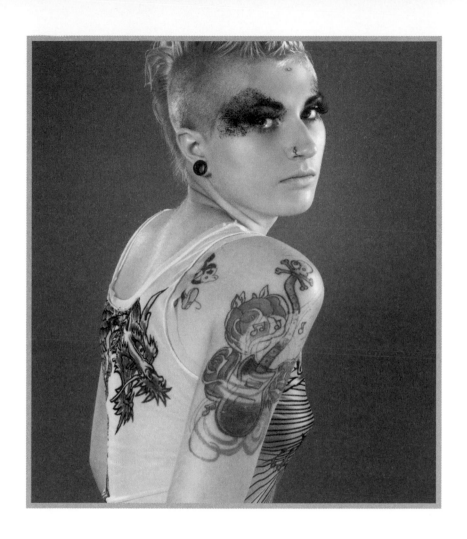

"Good tattoos are like a good marriage: you're proud of it and want to show it off… and you wake up to beauty every morning."

Terri Guillemets

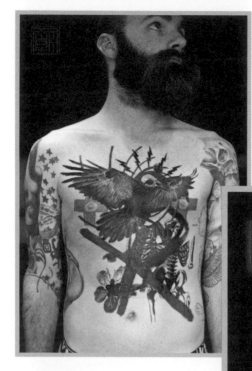

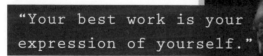

"Your best work is your expression of yourself."

Frank Gehry

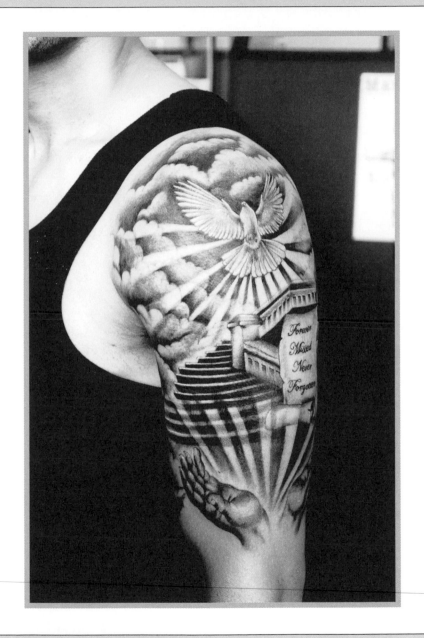

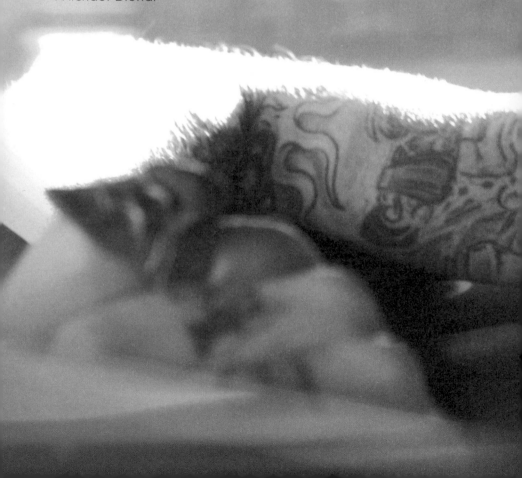

" Our bodies were printed as blank pages to be filled with the ink of our hearts. "

Michael Biondi

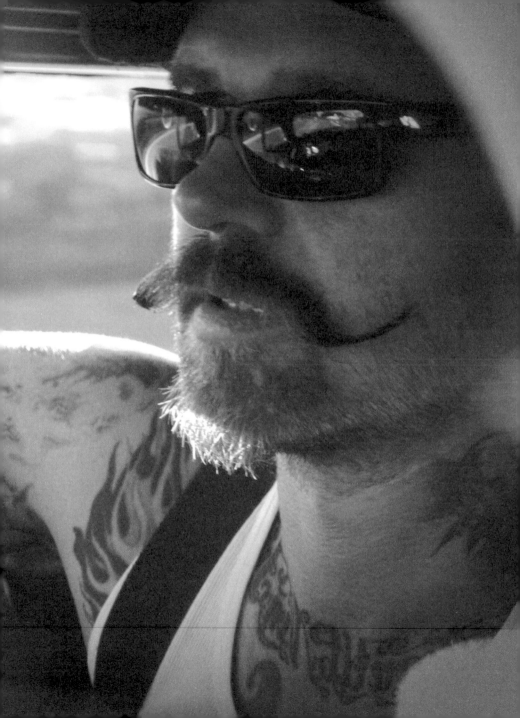

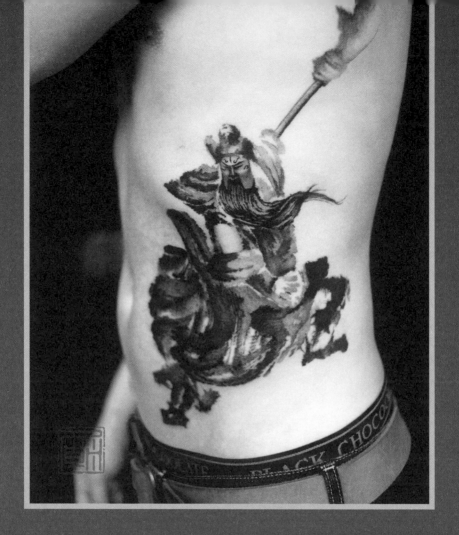

"Real painters understand with a brush
in their hand... what does anyone do
with rules? Nothing worthwhile."

Berthe Morisot

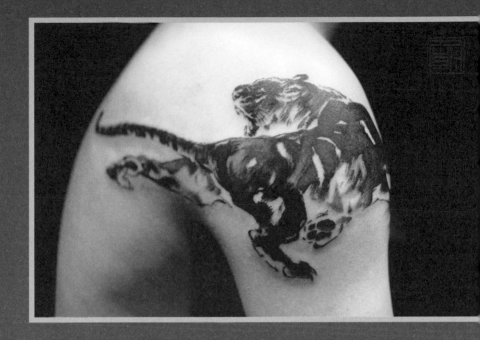

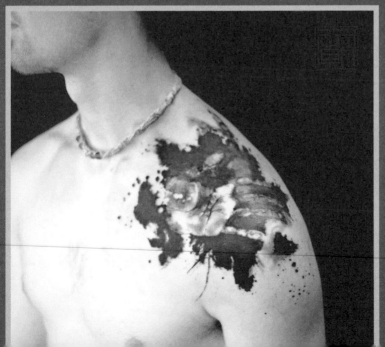

75

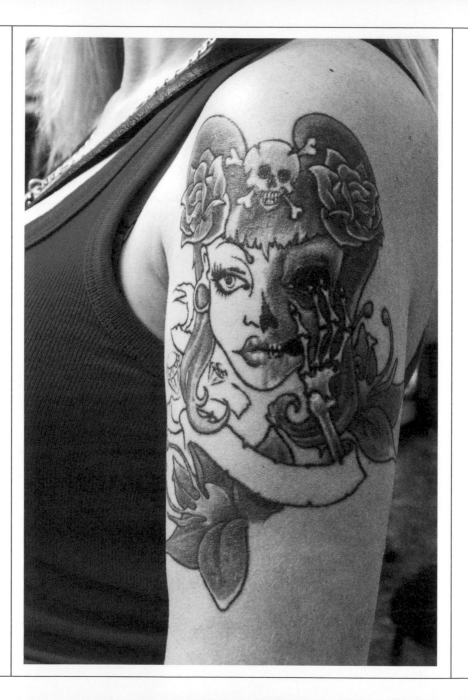

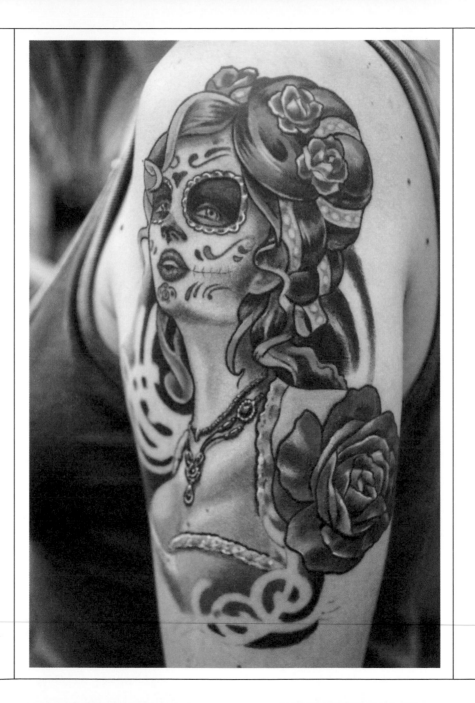

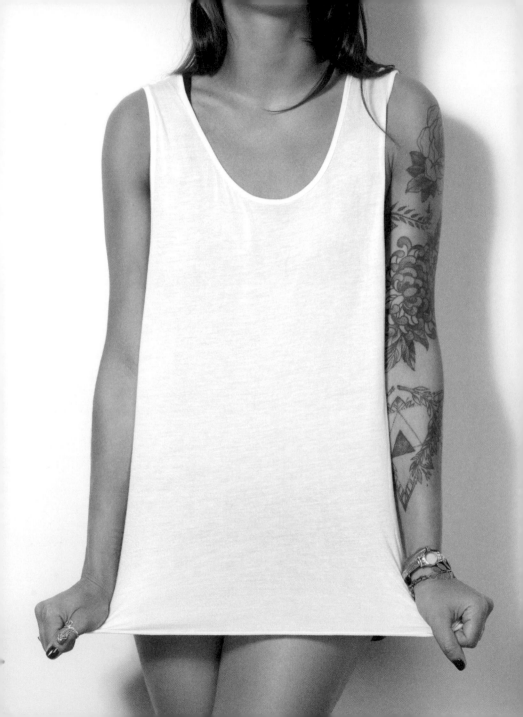

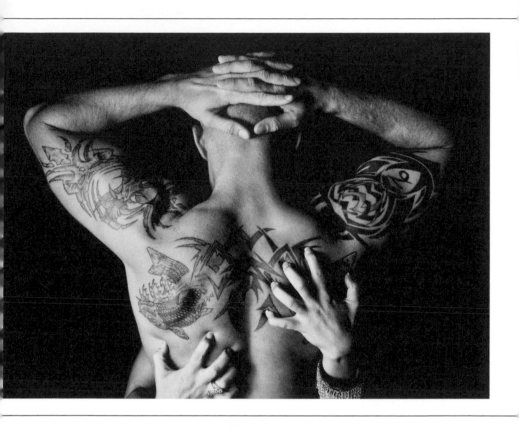

Fashion fades, only style
remains the same.

Coco Chanel

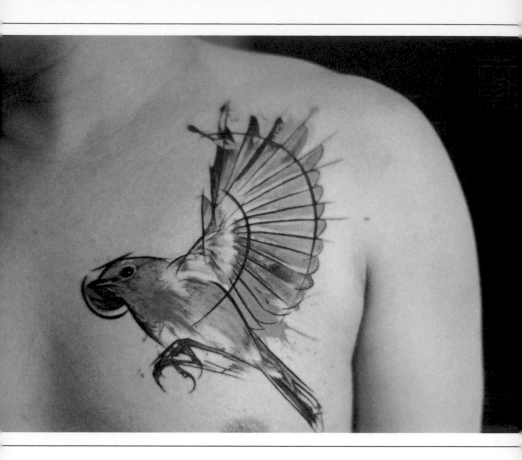

Refuse to be average. Let your heart soar as high as it will.

Aiden Wilson Tozer

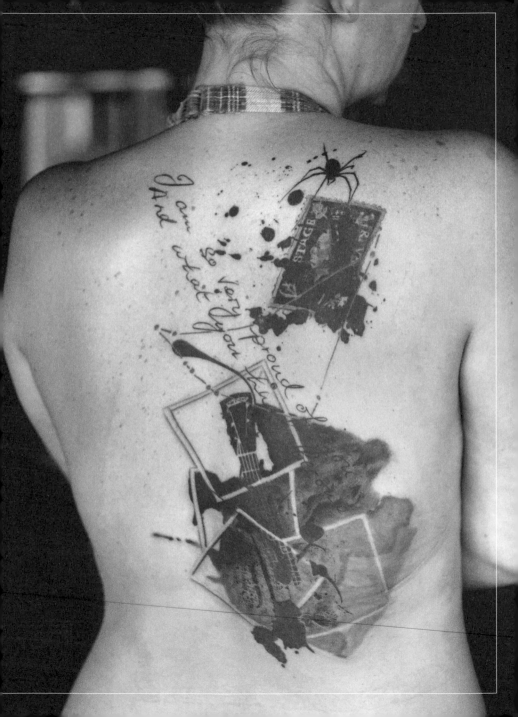

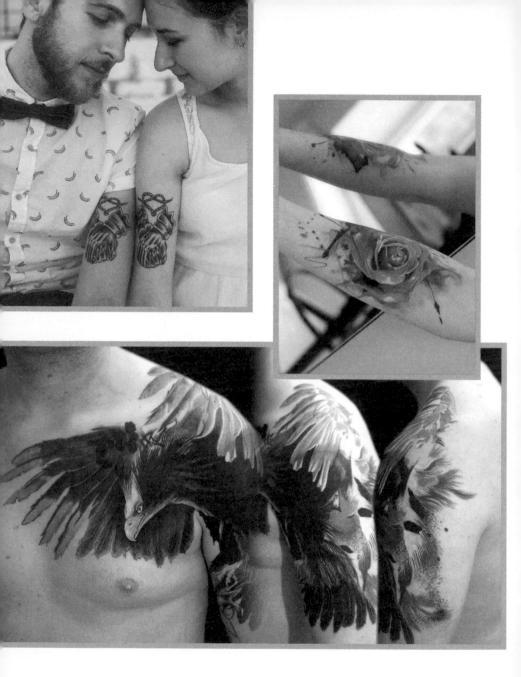

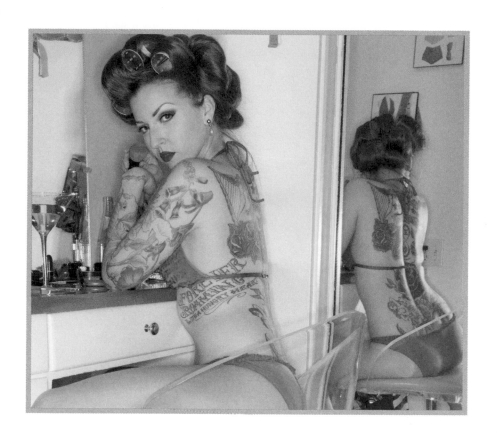

"Tattoos are like stories -
they're symbolic of the important
moments in your life."

Pamela Anderson

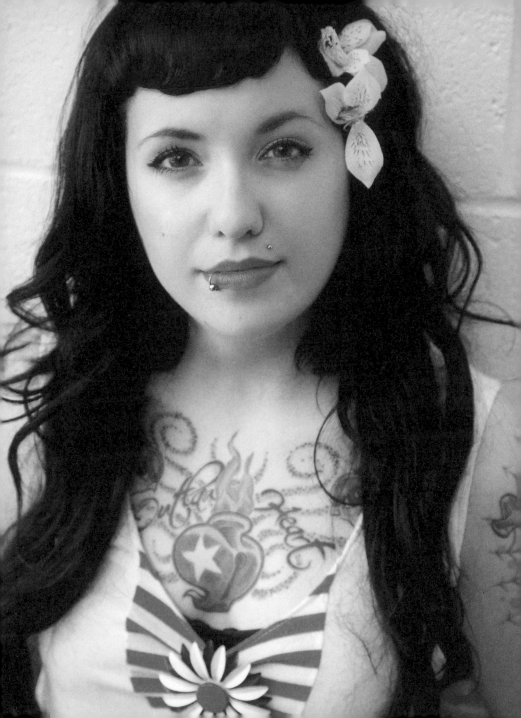

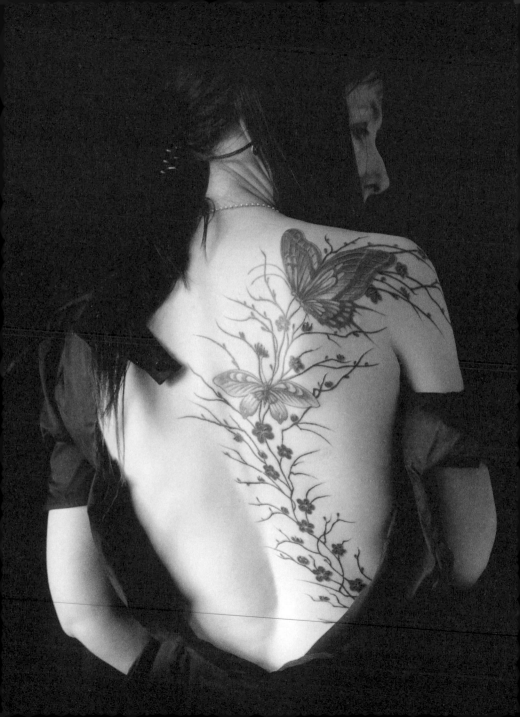

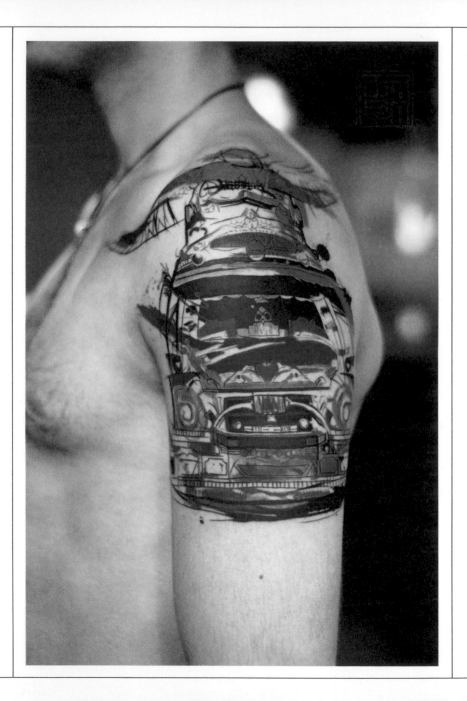

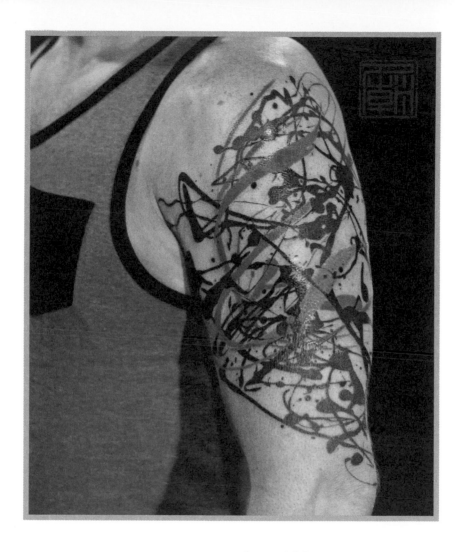

"Logic will get you from
A to B. Imagination will
take you everywhere."

Albert Einstein

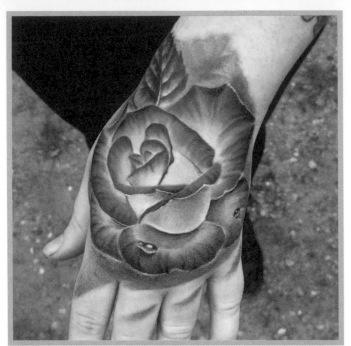

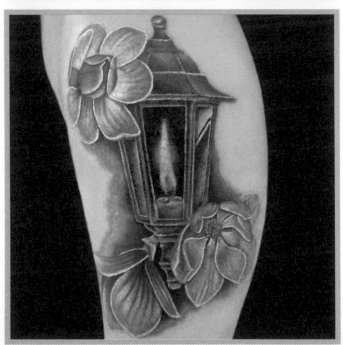

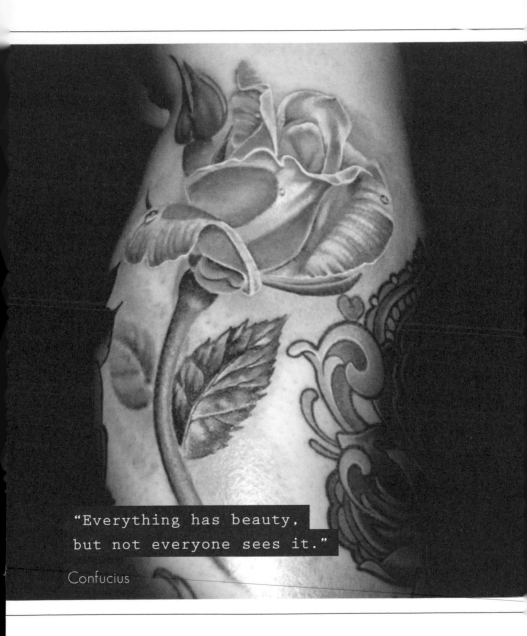

"Everything has beauty,
but not everyone sees it."

Confucius

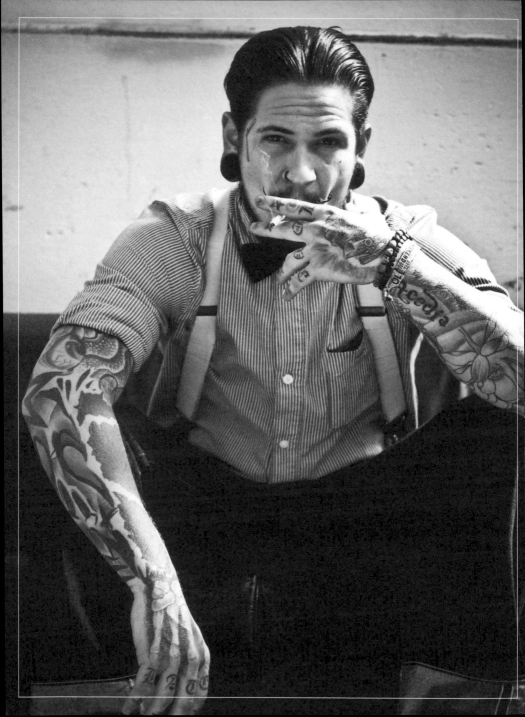

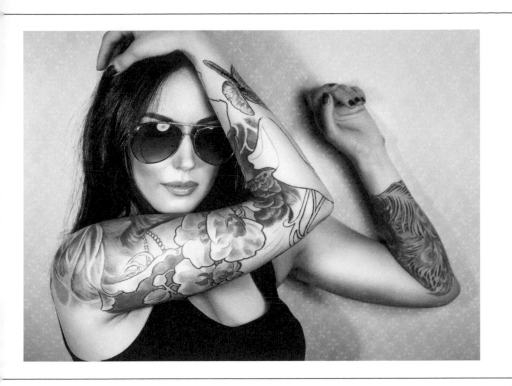

Life isn't about finding yourself.
Life is about creating yourself.

George Bernard Shaw

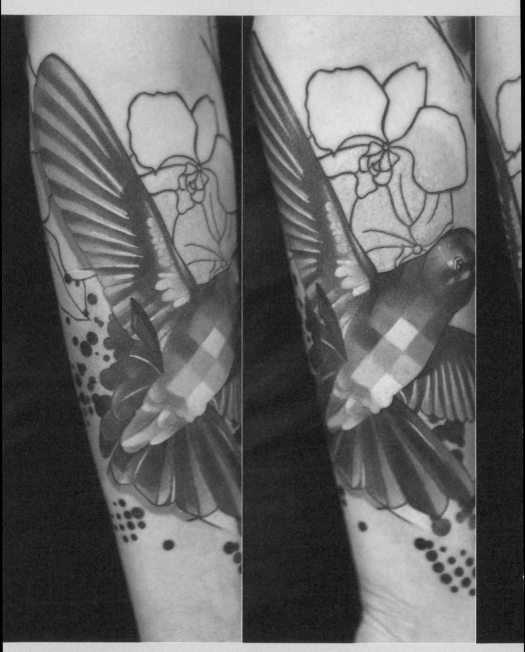

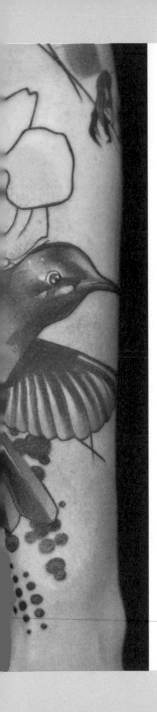

"Far away in the sunshine are my highest aspirations. I may not reach them, but I can look up and see the beauty, believe in them and try to follow where they lead. "

Louisa May Alcott

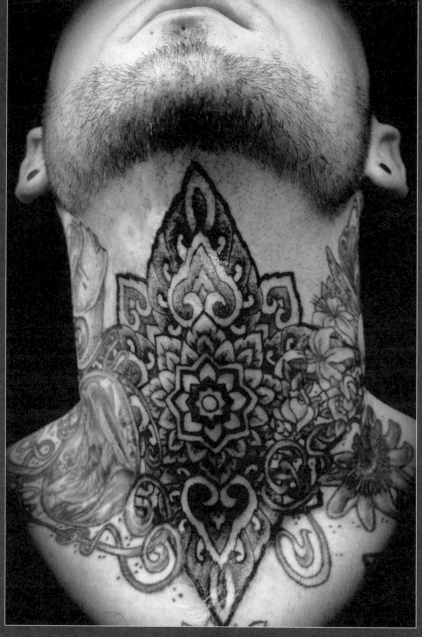

94

If you are not willing to risk the unusual, you will have to settle for the ordinary.

Jim Rohn

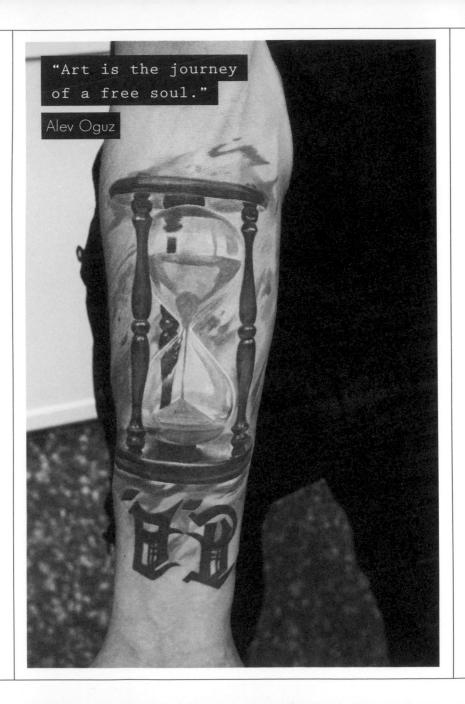

"Art is the journey of a free soul."

Alev Oguz

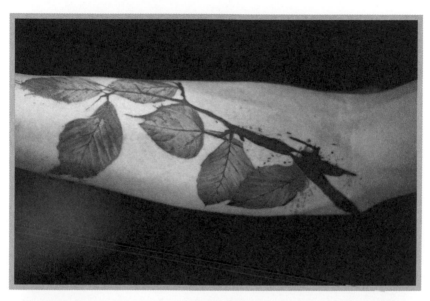

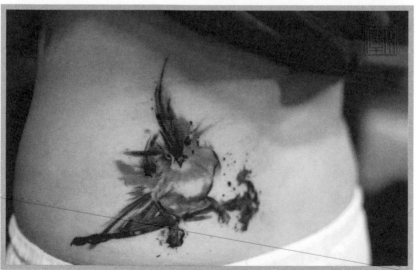

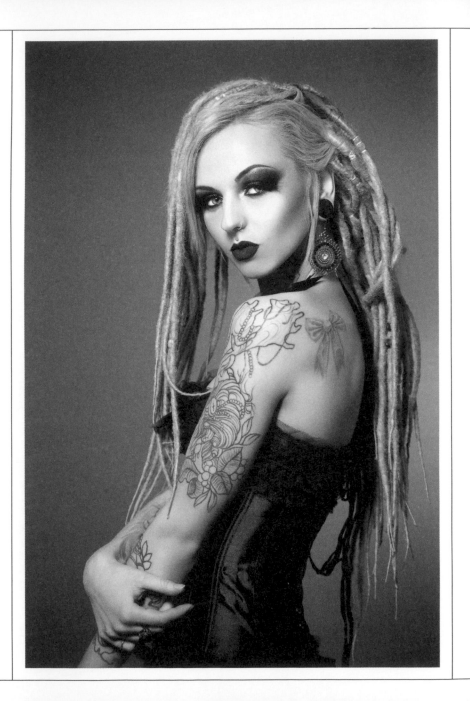

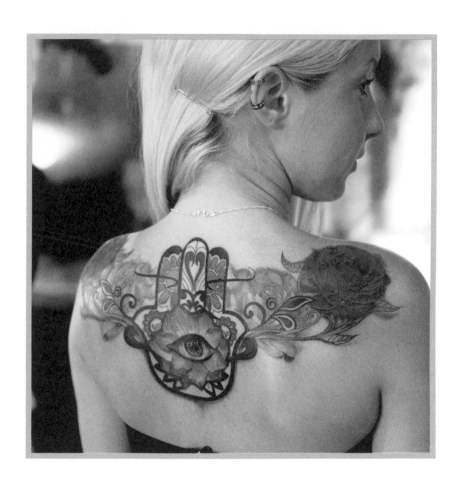

"I feel that the simplicity of
life is just being yourself."

Bobby Brown

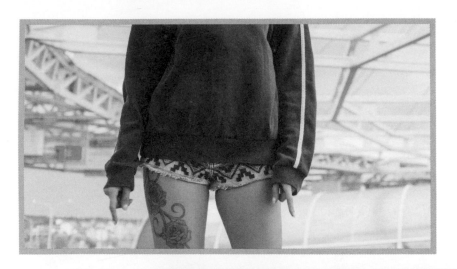

"Every production of an artist should be the expression of an adventure of his soul."

W. Somerset Maugham

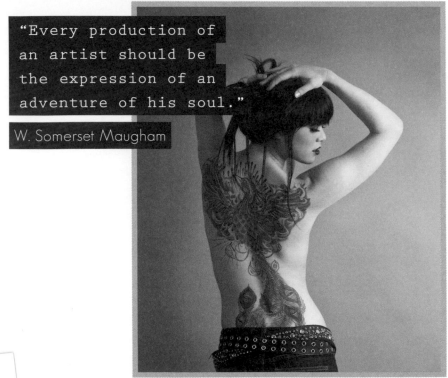

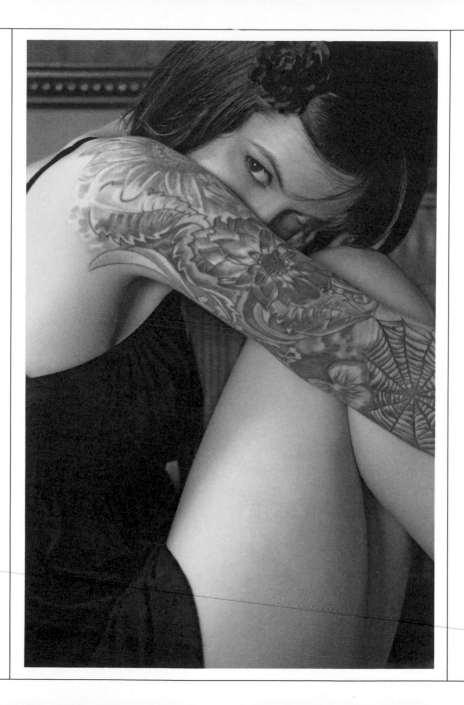

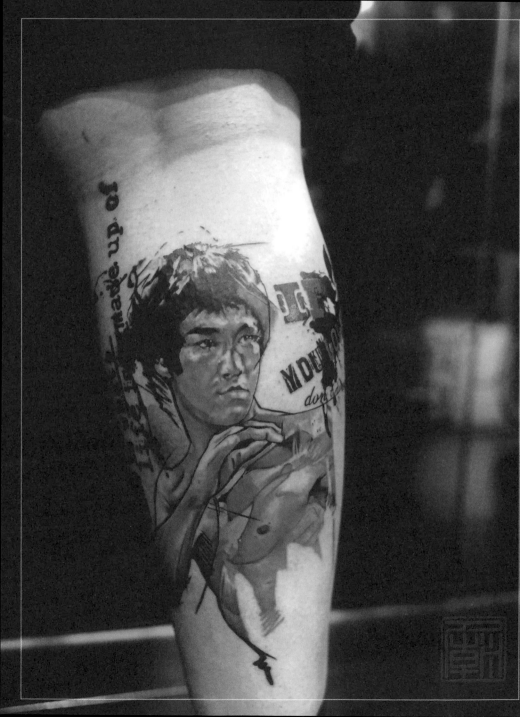

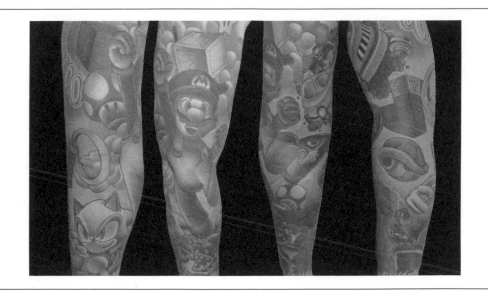

> ❝
> ──────────
>
> Moderation is a
> fatal thing; nothing
> succeeds like excess.
>
> Oscar Wilde
>
> ──────────
> ❞

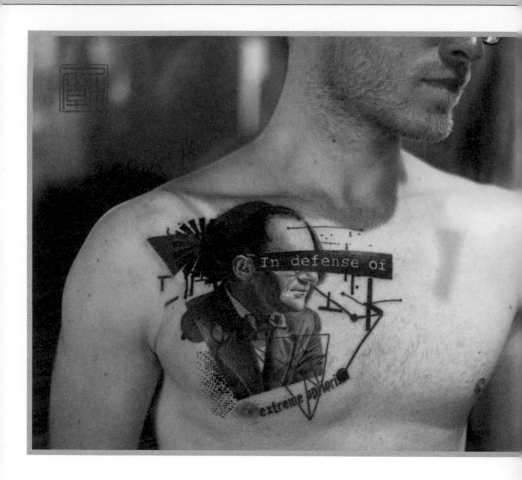

"Treasure the things
about you that make you
different and unique."

Karen Kain

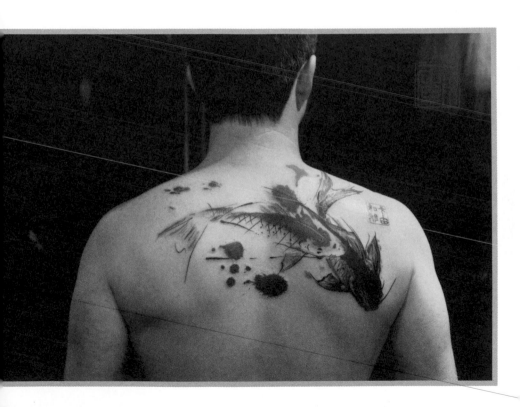

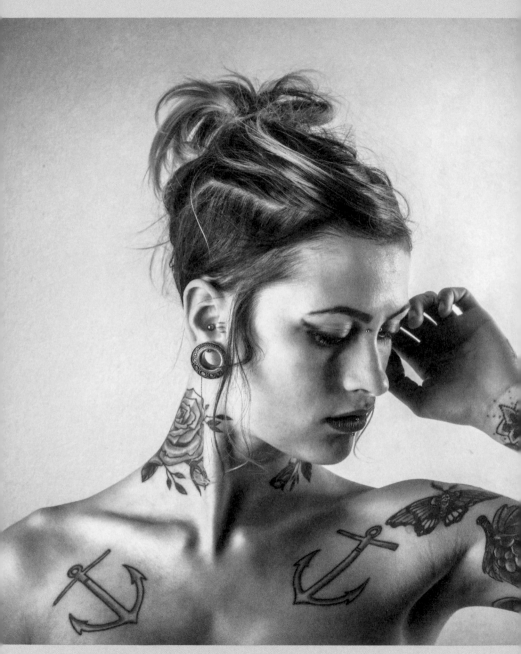

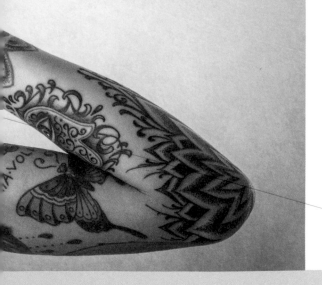

" A great tattoo is a statement, not a style. "

Vince Hemingson

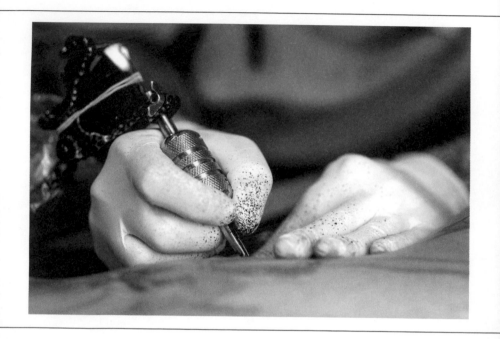

True creativity
often starts where
language ends.

Arthur Koestler

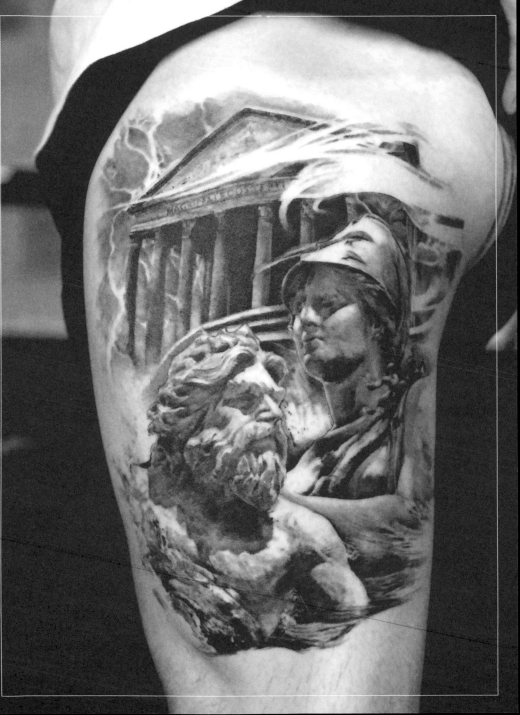

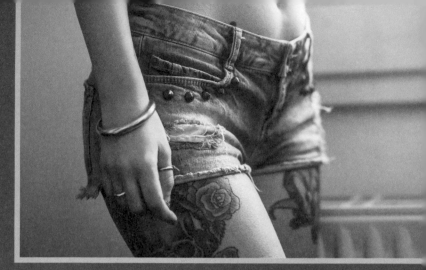

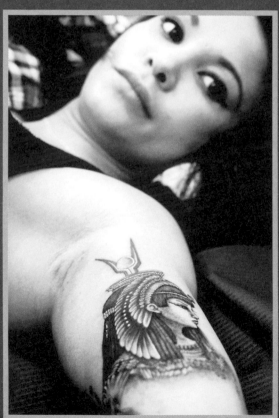

"Tattooing
is about
personalising
the body,
making it a
true home and
fit temple
for the spirit
that dwells
inside it."

Michelle Delio

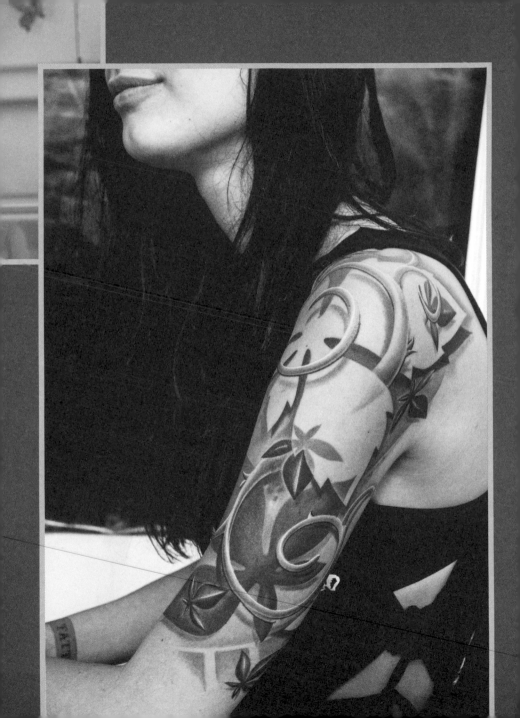

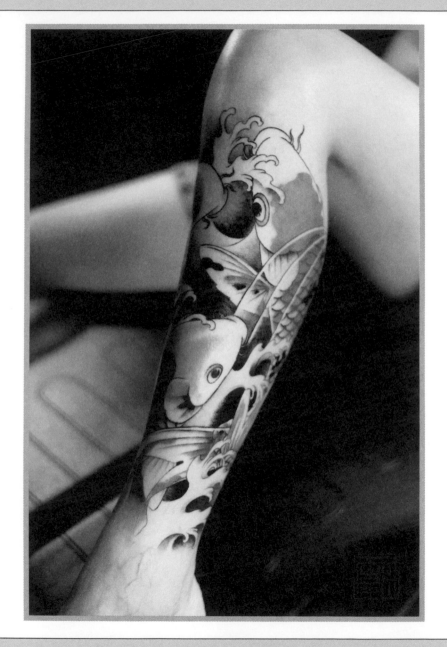
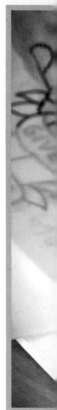

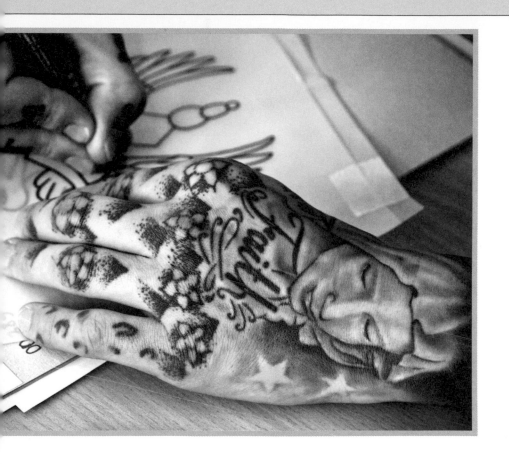

"Everything that happens
to us leaves some trace
behind; everything
contributes imperceptibly
to make us what we are."

Johann Wolfgang von Goethe

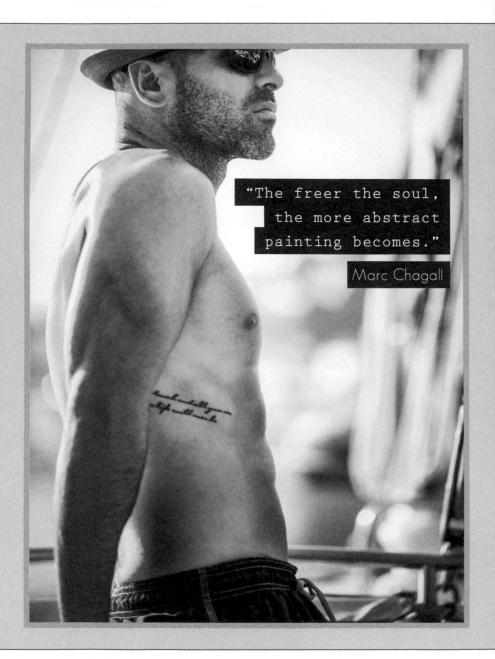

"The freer the soul,
the more abstract
painting becomes."

Marc Chagall

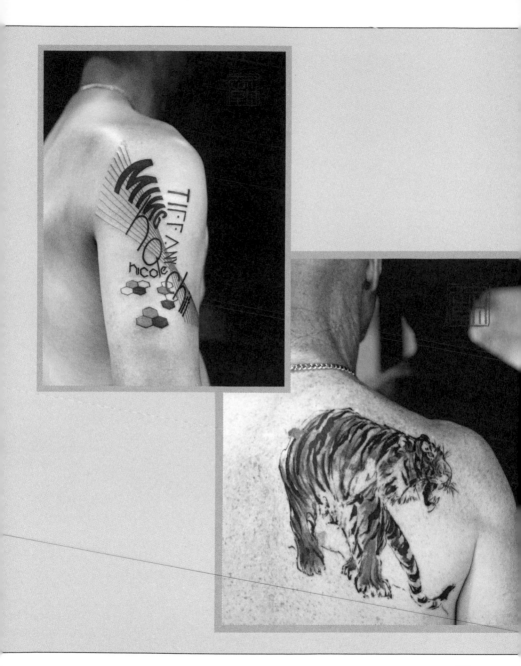

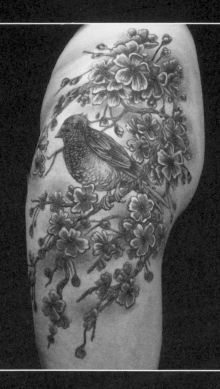

“

Beauty is skin deep.
A tattoo goes all the
way to the bone.

Vince Hemingson

”

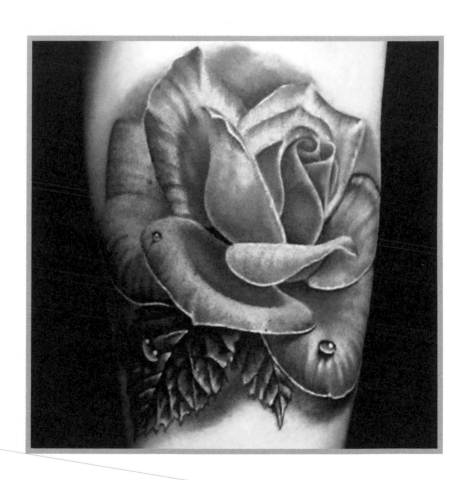

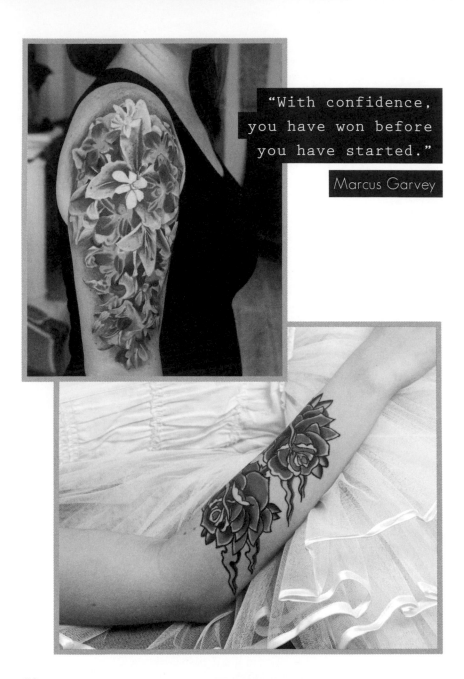

"With confidence,
you have won before
you have started."

Marcus Garvey

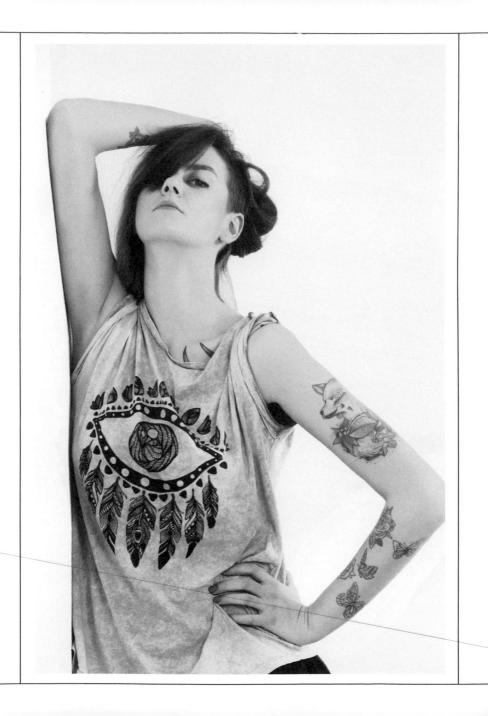

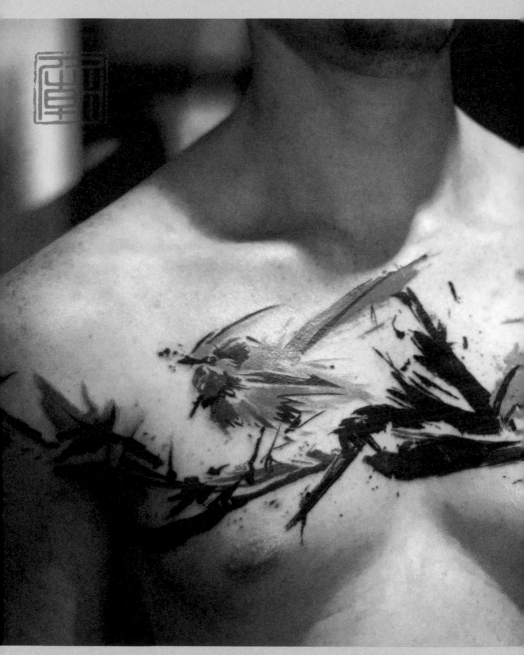

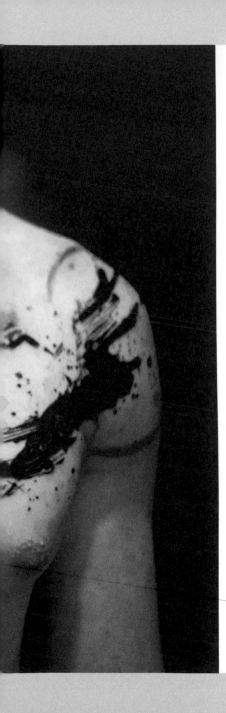

**❝ A work of
art is a
scream of
freedom. ❞**

Christo

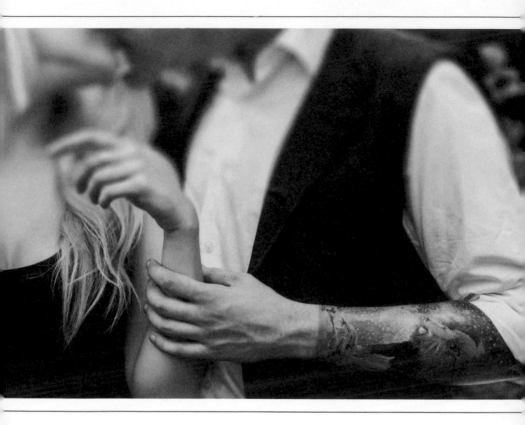

"

Glamour is a shooting star, it catches your
eye, but fades away; beauty is the sun,
always brilliant day after day.

Mike Dolan

"

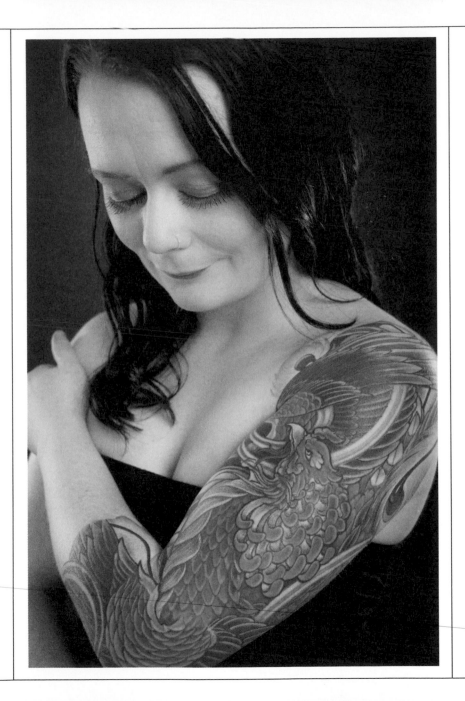

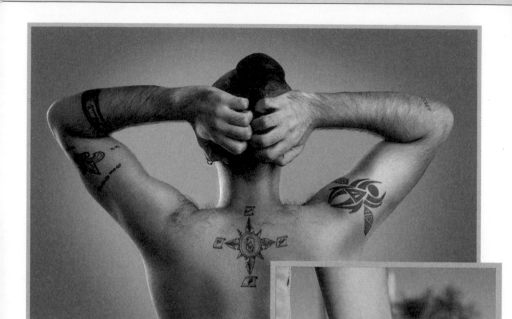

"It's only his
outside; a man
can be honest in
any sort of skin."

Herman Melville

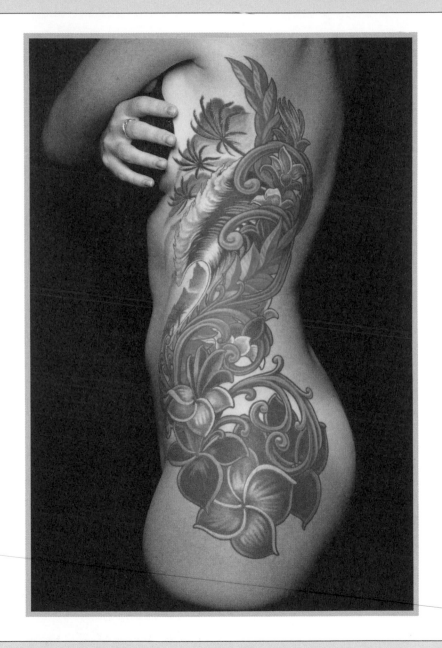

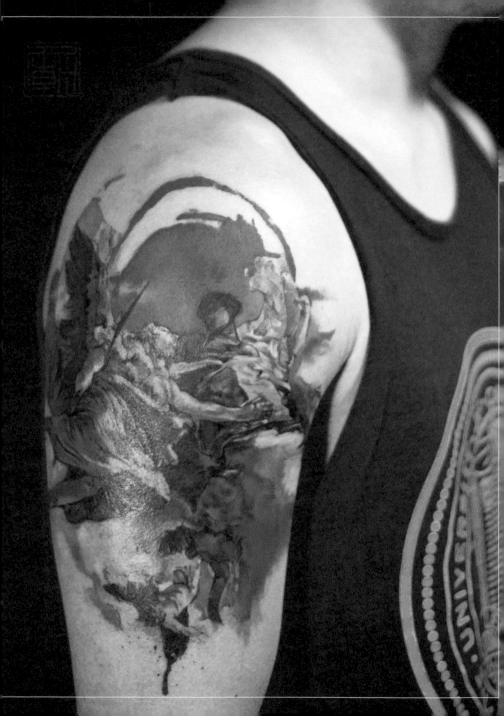

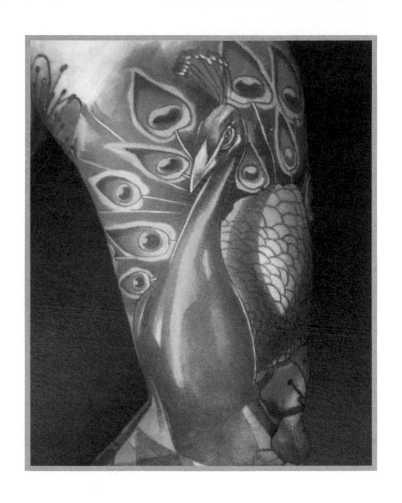

"The only person you have to please,
with your art, is yourself."

Don Getz

> **A man without tattoos is invisible to the Gods.**
>
> Iban proverb

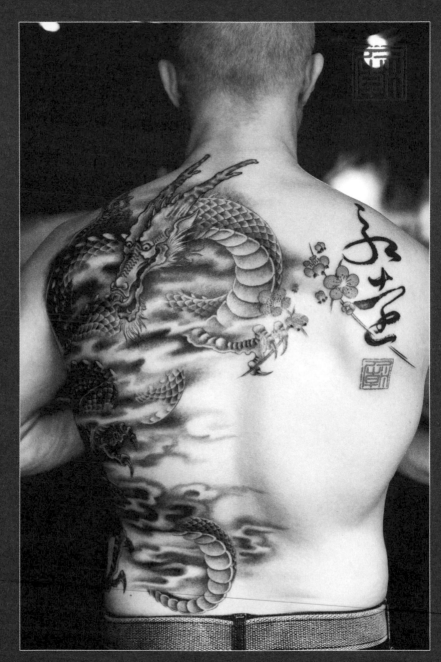

129

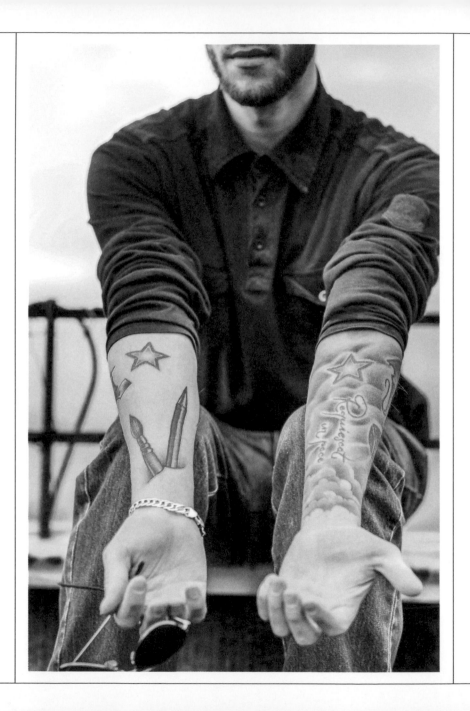

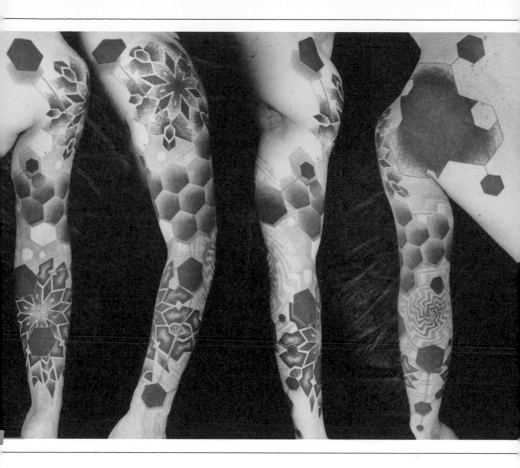

When I let go of what I am,
I become what I might be.

Lao Tzu

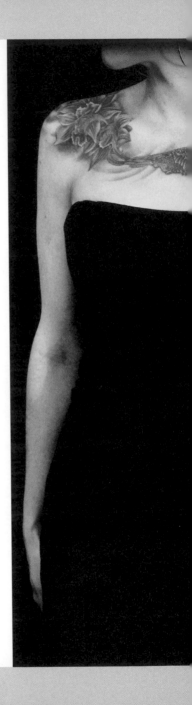

❝ Colours are brighter when the mind is open. ❞

Adriana Alarcon

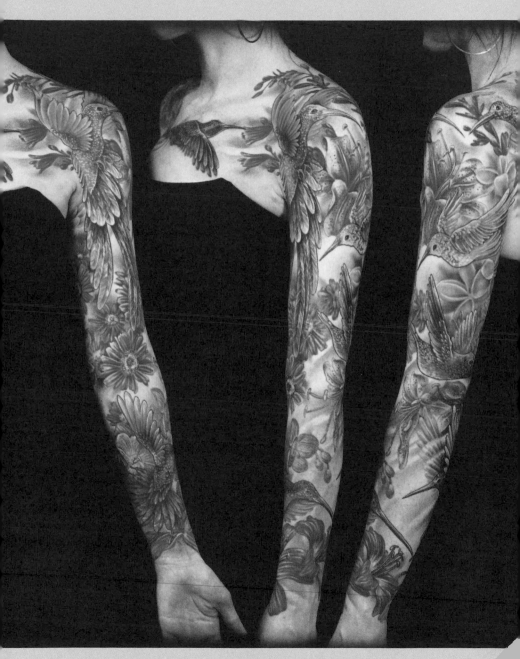

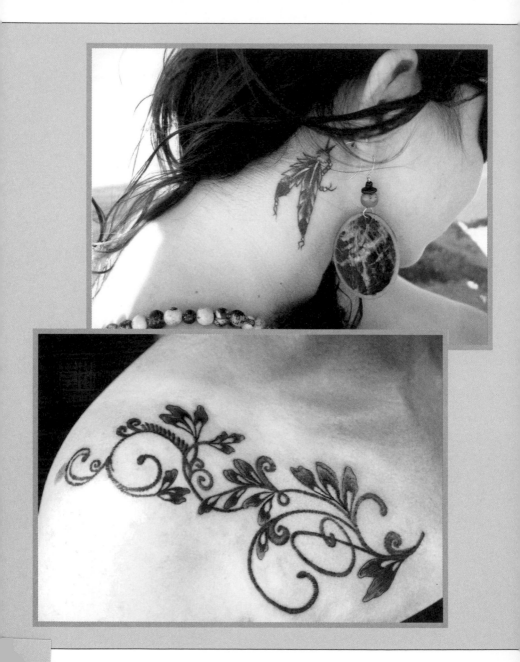

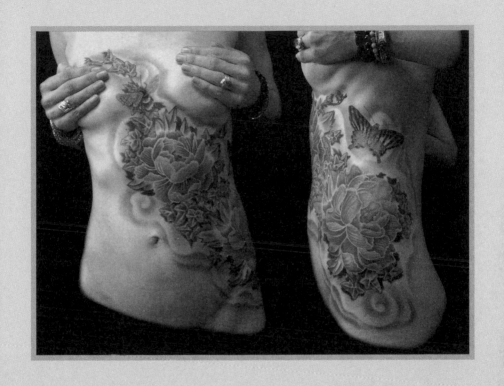

"The very best thing you can do for the whole world is to make the most of yourself."

Wallace Wattles

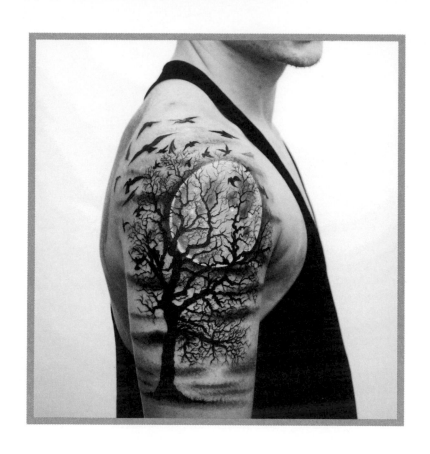

"A tattoo is a true poetic
creation, and is always
more than meets the eye."

V. Vale

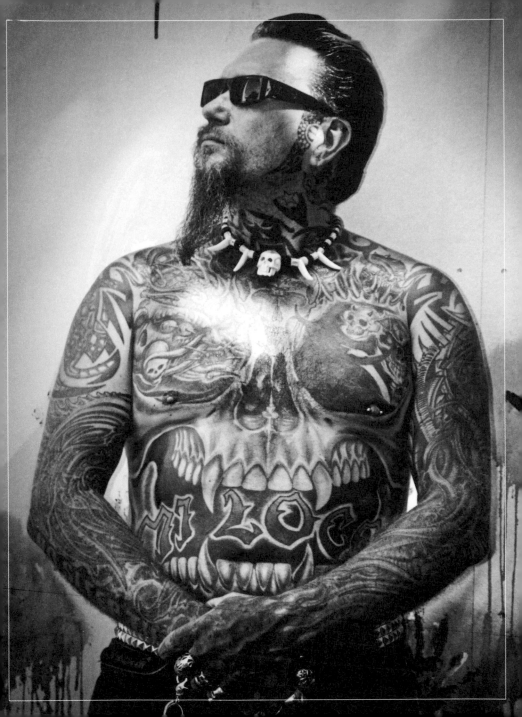

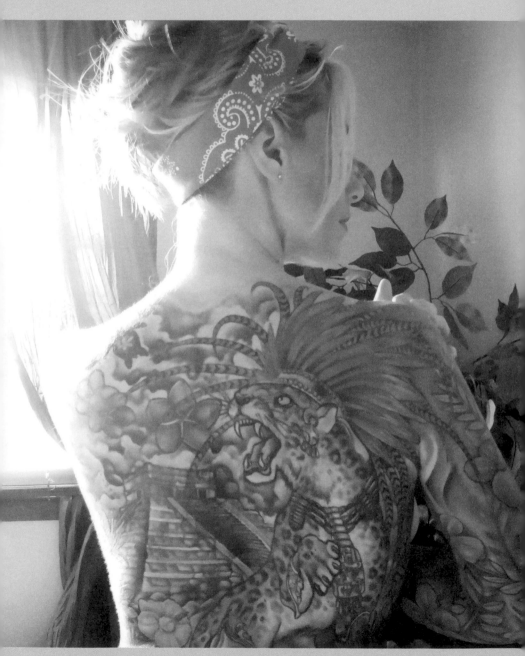

" In order to be irreplaceable one must always be different. "

Coco Chanel

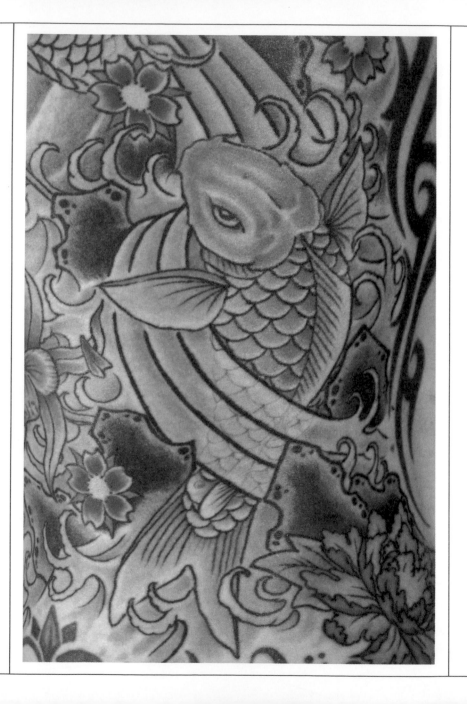

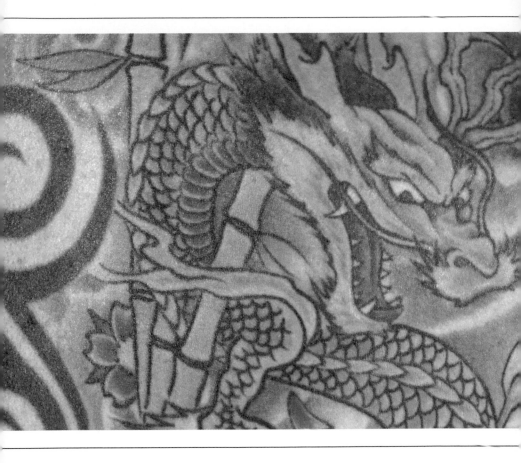

"The soul that is within
me no man can degrade."

Frederick Douglass

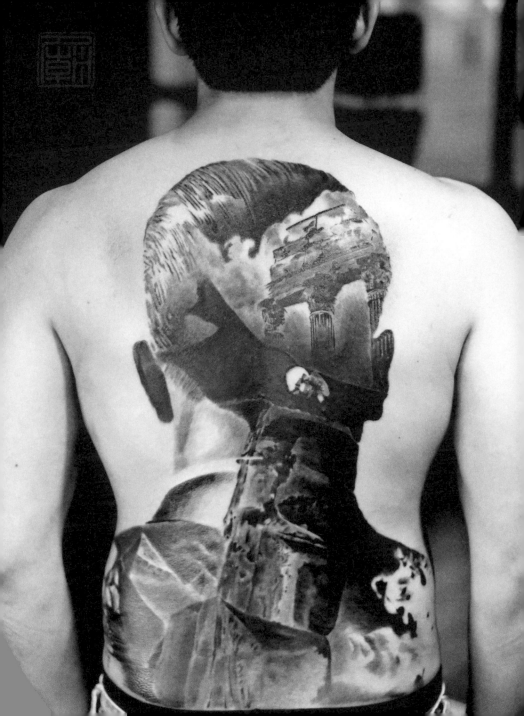

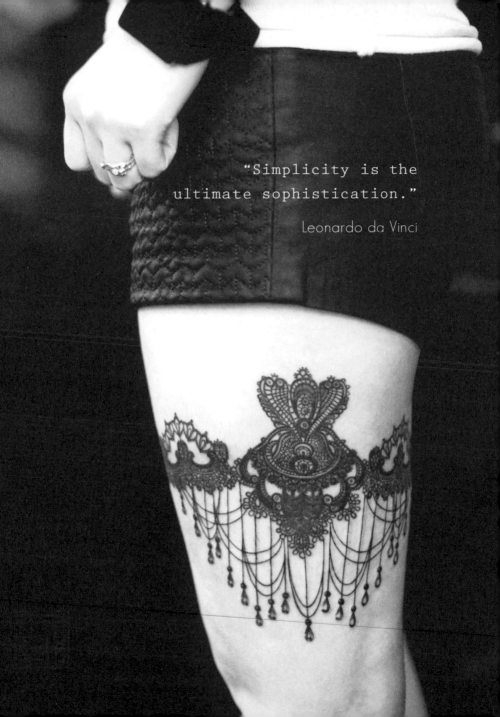

"Simplicity is the ultimate sophistication."

Leonardo da Vinci

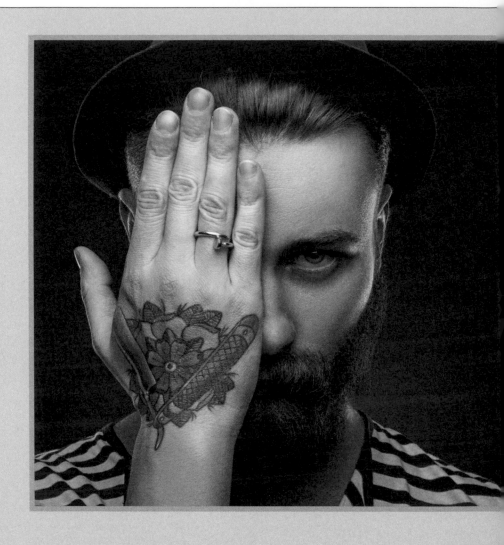

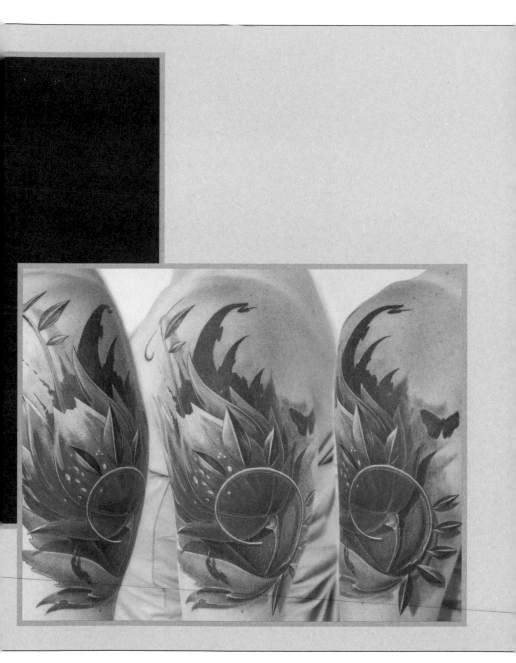

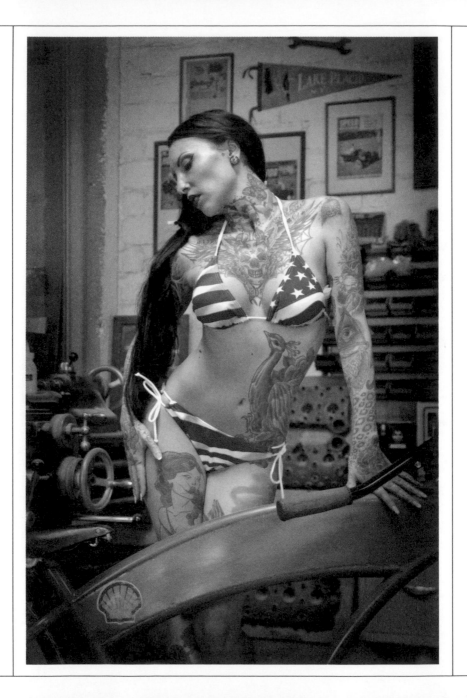

"Tattoos to me are the outward
symbol of the inward change
within my soul."

Nicolas Cage

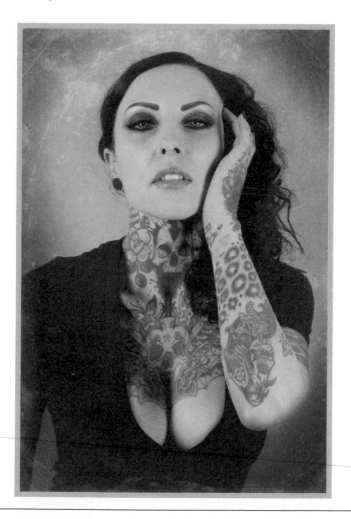

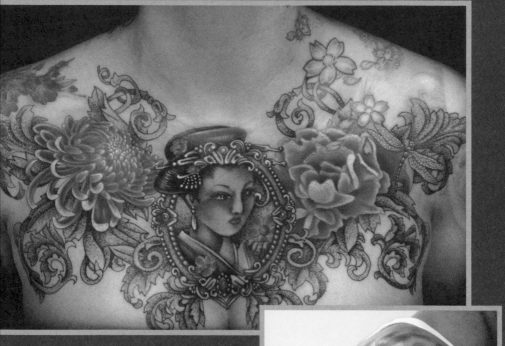

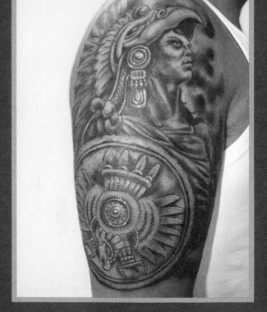

"What is genius
but the power of
expressing a new
individuality?"

Elizabeth Barrett
Browning

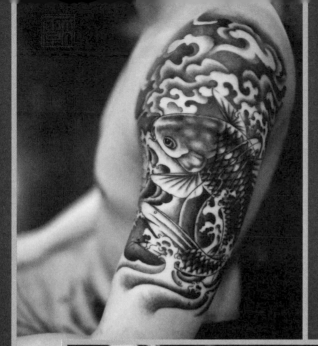

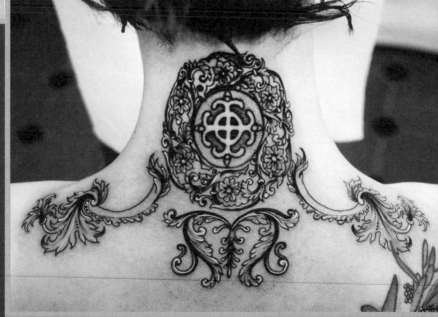

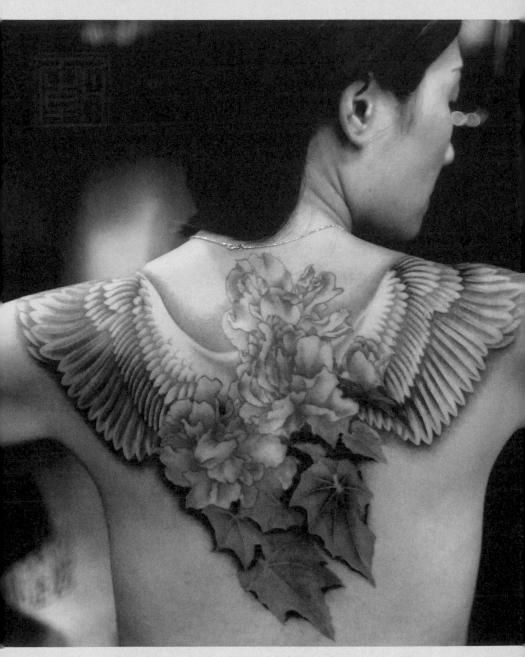

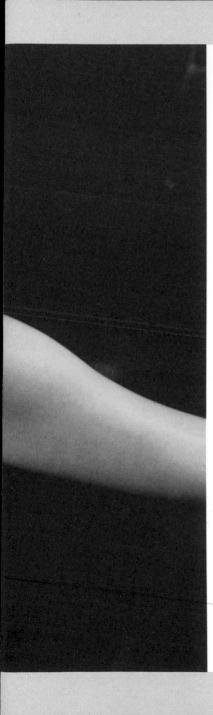

" And the day came when the risk to remain tight in a bud was more painful than the risk it took to blossom. 🥚

Anaïs Nin

"A bird does not
sing because it has
an answer. It sings
because it has a song."

Chinese proverb

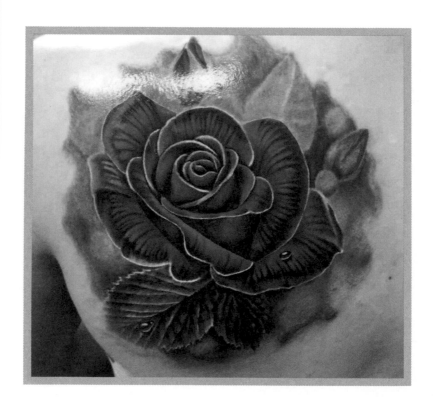

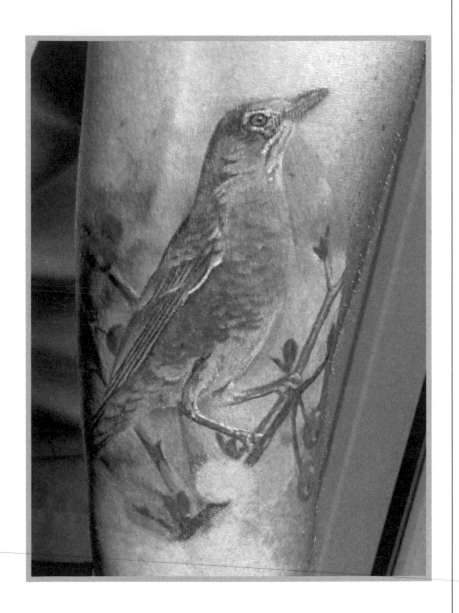

"Life has been your art. You have set yourself to music. Your days are your sonnets."

Oscar Wilde

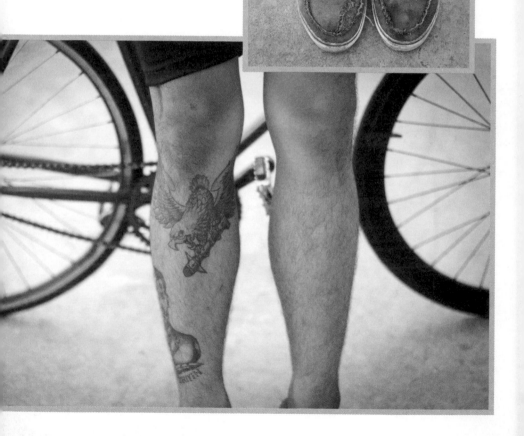

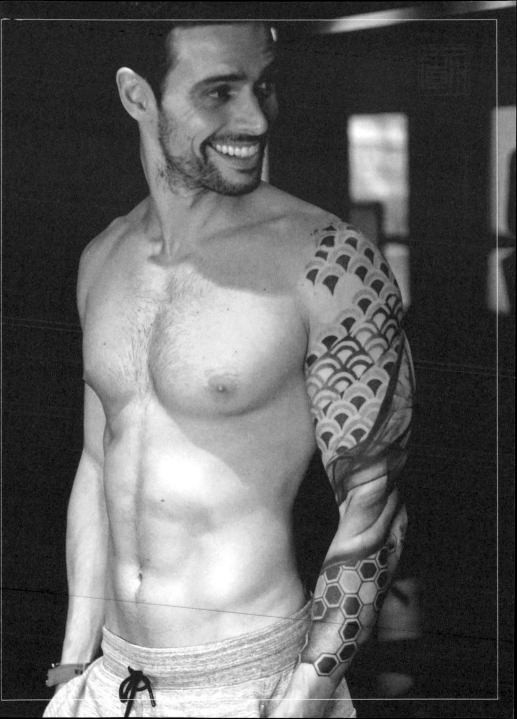

PHOTO CREDITS

A huge thank you to everybody who so generously contributed to this book.

Cover photo © Shutterstock
Back cover photos © Photographer: Dirk „The Pixeleye" Behlau / dirkbehlau.de Model: Andy Reisinger, True Fellas Tattoo
And Ivana Tattoo Art / ivanatattooart.com

p.4 – Photo © Shutterstock
p.6 – Photo © Photographer: Dirk „The Pixeleye" Behlau (dirkbehlau.de)
         Model: Christine Zimmer
p.8 – Photo © Joey Pang, Tattoo Temple, tattootemple.hk
p.9 – Photo © Joey Pang, Tattoo Temple, tattootemple.hk
p.10 – Photo © Liz Venom / lizvenom.com
p.11 – Photo © Liz Venom / lizvenom.com
p.12 – Photo © Shutterstock
p.13 – Photo © Shutterstock
p.14 – Photo © Shutterstock
p.15 – Photo © Shutterstock
p.16 – Photo © Shutterstock
p.17 – Left photo © Shutterstock
p.17 – Right photo © Jamie, Tattoo Temple, tattootemple.hk
p.18 – Top photo © Matt Shaver, Pussycat Tattoo Milwaukie, Oregon / pussycattattoo.com
p.18 – Bottom photo © Aaron Thompson
p.19 – Photo © Shutterstock
p.20 - Photo © Jamie, Tattoo Temple, tattootemple.hk
p.21 – Photo © Deanna Wardin / graphicward.com
p.22 – Photo © Elizabeth, Tattoo Temple, tattootemple.hk
p.23 – Photo © Elizabeth, Tattoo Temple, tattootemple.hk
p.24 – Photo © Shutterstock
p.26 – Top photo © Shutterstock
p.26 – Bottom photo © A. Aniñon / shotwithnikon.com
p.27 – Photo © Shutterstock
p.29 – Photo © Taguro Izumo / facebook.com/taguroizumoofficial
p.30 – Photo © Shutterstock
p.31 – Photo © Shutterstock
p.32 – Top photo © Wang, Tattoo Temple, tattootemple.hk
p.32 – Bottom photo © Wang, Tattoo Temple, tattootemple.hk
p.33 – Photo © Wang, Tattoo Temple, tattootemple.hk
p.34 – Photo © Shutterstock
p.35 – Photo © Shutterstock
p.36 – Photo © Liz Venom / lizvenom.com
p.37 – Top photo © Liz Venom / lizvenom.com
p.37 – Bottom photo © Liz Venom / lizvenom.com
p.38- Left photo © Elizabeth, Tattoo Temple, tattootemple.hk
p.38- Right photo © Elizabeth, Tattoo Temple, tattootemple.hk

p. 116 – Photo © Jo Harrison. Unlty Modern Body Art, UK / Unlty.tattoo

p. 117 – Photo © Liz Venom / lizvenom.com

p. 118 – Top photo © Miguel Angel / miguelangeltattoo.com

p. 118 – Bottom photo © Shutterstock

p. 119 – Photo © Shutterstock

p. 120 – Photo © Wang, Tattoo Temple, tattootemple.hk

p. 122 – Photo © Shutterstock

p. 123 – Photo © Jaime Valente

p. 124 – Top photo © Shutterstock

p. 124 – Bottom photo © Shutterstock

p. 125 – Photo © Champion Grubbs / championtattoo.com

p. 126 – Photo © Wang, Tattoo Temple, tattootemple.hk

p. 127 – Photo © Ivana Tattoo Art / ivanatattooart.com

p. 129 – Photo © Joey Pang, Tattoo Temple, tattootemple.hk

p. 130 – Photo © Shutterstock

p. 131 – Photo © Aleksandra Katsan /facebook.com/tattooedparadise

p. 132 – Photo © Jo Harrison. Unlty. Modern Body Art, UK / Unlty.tattoo

p. 134 – Top photo © Priscilla Macedo

p. 134 – Bottom photo © Elizabeth, Tattoo Temple, tattootemple.hk

p. 135 – Photo © Jo Harrison. Unlty. Modern Body Art, UK / Unlty.tattoo

p. 136 – Photo © Miguel Angel / miguelangeltattoo.com

p. 137 – Photo © Photographer: Dirk „The Pixeleye" Behlau / dirkbehlau.de
         Model: Ski King, Singer

p. 138 – Photo © Jennifer Guizar

p. 140 – Photo © Shutterstock

p. 141 – Photo © Shutterstock

p. 142 – Photo © Jamie, Tattoo Temple, tattootemple.hk

p. 143 – Photo © Olivia, Tattoo Temple, tattootemple.hk

p. 144 – Photo © Shutterstock

p. 145 – Photo © Aleksandra Katsan /facebook.com/tattooedparadise

p. 146 – Photo © Photographer: Dirk „The Pixeleye" Behlau / dirkbehlau.de
         Model: Makani Terror

p. 147 – Photo © Photographer: Dirk „The Pixeleye" Behlau / dirkbehlau.de
         Model: Makani Terror

p. 148 – Top photo © Jo Harrison. Unlty. Modern Body Art, UK / Unlty.tattoo

p. 148 – Bottom photo © Ray Wewerka, Flaming Art Tattoo / flamingarttattoo.com

p. 149 – Top photo © Joey Pang, Tattoo Temple, tattootemple.hk

p. 149 – Bottom photo © Miguel Angel / miguelangeltattoo.com

p. 150 – Photo © Joey Pang, Tattoo Temple, tattootemple.hk

p. 152 – Photo © Liz Venom / lizvenom.com

p. 153 – Photo © Liz Venom / lizvenom.com

p. 154 – Top photo © Shutterstock

p. 154 – Bottom photo © Shutterstock

p. 155 – Photo © Jamie, Tattoo Temple, tattootemple.hk

"Tattoos decorate the
body but they also
enhance the soul."

Michelle Delio